1983

IMAGES AND CONVERSATIONS

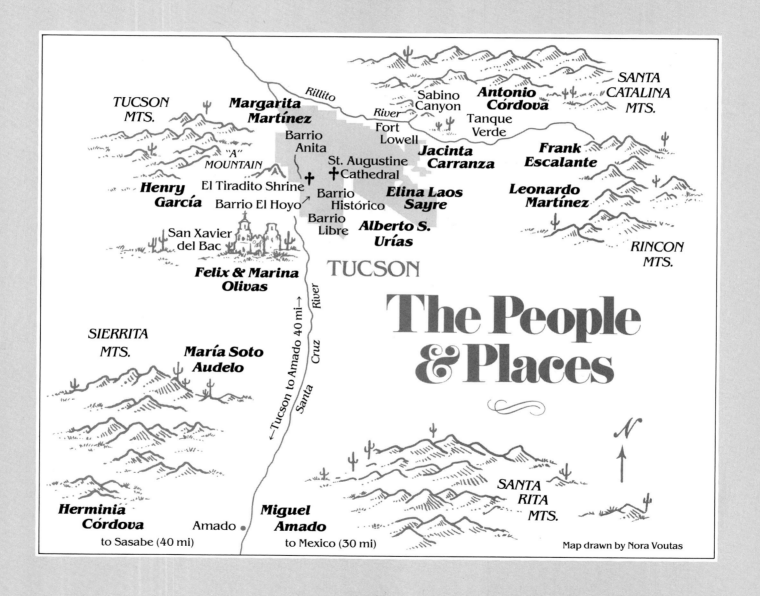

TUCSON MTS.

Rillito

Margarita Martínez

River

Fort Lowell

Sabino Canyon

Antonio Córdova

SANTA CATALINA MTS.

Tanque Verde

Barrio Anita

St. Augustine Cathedral

Jacinta Carranza

Frank Escalante

"A" MOUNTAIN

Henry García

El Tiradito Shrine

Barrio El Hoyo

Barrio Histórico

Elina Laos Sayre

Leonardo Martínez

Barrio Libre

San Xavier del Bac

Alberto S. Urías

RINCON MTS.

Felix & Marina Olivas

TUCSON

The People & Places

SIERRITA MTS.

María Soto Audelo

Tucson to Amado 40 mi →

Santa Cruz River

← Tucson to Amado 40 mi

SANTA RITA MTS.

Herminia Córdova

Amado •

Miguel Amado

N ↑

to Sasabe (40 mi)

to Mexico (30 mi)

Map drawn by Nora Voutas

IMAGES AND CONVERSATIONS

Mexican Americans Recall a Southwestern Past

PATRICIA PRECIADO MARTIN

Photographs by
LOUIS CARLOS BERNAL

THE UNIVERSITY OF ARIZONA PRESS

TUCSON, ARIZONA

About the Author...

PATRICIA PRECIADO MARTIN, a native Arizonan, has been a collector of local history and folktales for several years and has served as a consultant to a number of history projects dealing with the Mexican-American presence in the Southwest. A magna cum laude graduate of the University of Arizona, Martin has published numerous articles and a bilingual children's book, *The Bellringer of San Agustín* (Pajarito Publications, 1980).

About the Photographer...

LOUIS CARLOS BERNAL, also a native Arizonan, has received numerous awards and honors for his photography, among them two Mexican-American Legal Defense and Education Fund grants and a 1980 National Endowment for the Arts Fellowship. Bernal, who earned his B.A. and M.F.A. degrees at Arizona State University, has taught courses in design and photography at Pima Community College in Tucson.

THE UNIVERSITY OF ARIZONA PRESS

Copyright © 1983
The Arizona Board of Regents
All Rights Reserved

This book was set in 11/13 V-I-P Century Oldstyle
Manufactured in the U.S.A.

Library of Congress Cataloging in Publication Data

Martin, Patricia Preciado.
    Images and conversations.

    1. Mexican Americans—Arizona—Tucson Region—
Biography.   2. Tucson Region (Ariz.)—Biography.
3. Mexican Americans—Arizona—Tucson Region—Social
conditions.   4. Tucson Region (Ariz.)—Social
conditions. I. Bernal, Louis Carlos. II. Title.
F819.T99M55   1983   979.1'77   83-1186
ISBN 0-8165-0801-1
ISBN 0-8165-0803-8 (pbk.)

To the Memory of My Mother,
Aurelia Romero Preciado

CONTENTS

The House
of the Fig Tree

In 1910 Leonardo Martínez left a pattern of his footprints in the mud adobe bricks his father was drying in the summer sun. His father, Jesús María Martínez, was to use those same bricks to build their humble home in one of Tucson, Arizona's oldest Mexican neighborhoods, Barrio Anita. It was a home which in spite of time and urban sprawl still was standing in the 1980s, a graceful reminder of another era, a home still occupied by the descendants of Jesús María Martínez—another testimony to the strength of the legacy left by the family patriarch. "If you knock down those walls," says Leonardo Martínez, "you would still find my little footprints in those adobes—70 years later."

It is tempting to ponder that on the stillest of nights, the sounds of a child running and jumping can still be heard echoing in the walls of that barrio home. The pitter-patter of little feet carried to its poetic extreme.

In 1858, José M. Sosa built a small residence for his family on Main Street—Tucson's old Camino Real—the Spanish king's Royal Highway. In 1878 the property was sold to Leopoldo Carrillo, who enlarged the home for his family. In time he dug a well, built corrals and chicken houses, planted herbs and flowers—and a fig tree. The fig tree, nourished by the sweet water drawn from the well, flourished in that desert garden. Through the years it grew, its spreading branches finally embracing the garden wall. On warm summer nights, the family would gather outdoors to enjoy the cool evening breeze. Undisturbed by the noise or concerns of modern urbanites, they would count the stars and fall asleep beneath the protective canopy of the sky and the fig tree.

Through the years the fig tree continued to grow and give fruit to succeeding generations. In the twentieth century a bustling Mexican neighborhood grew up around the house of the fig tree. It was a community of vitality and culture and tradition, built with the love and labor of those who dwelled there. But the laughter and songs of the descendants of those early Mexican pioneers would in time be silenced by the bulldozers of progress and urban renewal. Only the Sosa-Carrillo house* would be spared, standing alone in a wilderness of asphalt, brick, and glass—mute evidence of the past. And miraculously that same fig tree still branched and flowered in stubborn affirmation of those families who gave it root, greening forth in solitude—a symbol of history and nostalgia in a modern waste-land of concrete, an inheritance which still gives sustenance to those of us who pass this way.

But although the bulldozer can destroy neighborhoods, it cannot erase memory. Progress can obliterate monuments, but it cannot destroy the spirit and strength of a people. The oral history collection presented in this book—the personal reminiscences, folktales, anecdotes, and traditions—is an intimate narrative of Tucson's Mexican-American pioneers, whose ancestors planted traditions as well as trees, who impressed values as well as footprints. It is a story told in the voice of the people which is evocative of the Hispanic presence in all of the Southwest, whether in San Antonio, Santa Fe, Pueblo, Colorado, or Los Angeles. Those footprints have left paths upon which we travel. Those trees have left branches which give us shelter from a technological world we don't always understand.

It is hoped that this book will inspire all who read it to search for their history. Trees that were given root and footsteps that were implanted are a legacy we all share, regardless of our ethnicity. It matters not whether it is a twisting fig tree in Arizona or a gnarled apple tree in the Ohio Valley; the Camino Real or Santa Fe Trail in the Southwest or the Lewis and Clark Trail in the Northwest; we yearn and we ask the questions: Who am I? From whence did I come? What are my roots? In whose footsteps do I walk? We search not just for bloodlines and dusty mementos and faded photographs, but for the shape of our values and our souls.

---

*Located in the center of Tucson's Community Center complex, the house became a branch museum of the Arizona Heritage Center, known as the Frémont House after the Territorial governor John Frémont, who rented and occupied it for a few months in 1880. The naming of the house generated much protest among the city's Hispanic community, which believed that the house should have been given the name which most accurately reflected its owners and history.

This book attempts to answer some of those questions. It speaks of the spirit and values of another time when people lingered. It was a time when relationships were one to one, whether with a neighbor or with the elements or with a seedling or with God. It was a time of independence and self-reliance and faith. People built their own homes. They raised their own barns and their own food and their own children. They marked out their territories and decided on the parameters of their world. They planted trees so that their grandchildren could climb among their branches and so that their descendants could pick the fruit. The people stayed.

And finally, this book attempts to teach us to listen. In a time when youth and innovation and change are valued over age and wisdom and permanence, we must learn again to listen to the songs taught to us by our elders.

For the history of all people is a treasure which is there for the asking—not one to be found buried and gleaming in sunken ships or abandoned mines, but a history found in richness of culture and oral tradition. It must be sought with diligence and patience and affection. It must be collected with love and when the occasion arises—on sidewalk stoops, on church steps, on nostalgic walks, on garden benches, at kitchen tables sipping coffee.

Above the din of the computer and the television and the roar of space-age engines, there is a voice sweet and simple, but true. It teaches us about ourselves. It teaches the old songs. And those songs bear repeating.

I would like to thank all the individuals and families who opened their doors as well as their hearts to us while we were gathering material for this book. Without their generosity and trust, our work would not have been possible. Thanks also to Jim and Sandy for the patience, good humor, and encouragement they exhibited, and to the University of Arizona Press for bringing about the publication of this book.

P. P. M.

ANTONIO CORDOVA

& The Tanque Verde & Sabino Canyon

My name is Antonio Córdova. I was born in a house on Convent and 17th on January 26, 1903. On my mother's side of the family, we have been in Tucson for five generations. My great-grandmother's name was Pantaleona Ayala. She had a house on 17th and Main, about two lots to the north of the corner. Of course, that house does not exist anymore. My mother, Antonia Valenzuela, was born in that house on September 2, 1876. My grandfather's name was Damean Valenzuela and my grandmother's name was Eutimia Ayala. At first they were not settled in any one place because he was a *tahur* (card dealer; gambler), and they used to travel from fiesta to fiesta. They would come here to the Fiesta de San Agustín* and then go to the fiesta in Magdalena, and so on. After they began to have a family they settled more permanently and bought the corner of 17th and Meyer—across from Jerry's Lee Ho Market—where they built a house.

The Fiesta de San Agustín used to be held in Levin's Park**—it used to be located where all the government buildings are now. I guess it was like the fiestas are now—sell a little here, sell a little there. Of course, the laws were not so strict as they are now, and there used to be a lot of drinking and gambling. At least that's

---

*The fiesta honoring St. Augustine, the patron saint of Tucson, was the major social event in the city's early history. It was a colorful celebration, both religious and secular in nature. It began on August 28, the saint's feast day, and ended on September 16, Mexican Independence Day. The fiesta attracted hundreds of visitors and merchants from throughout the Southwest and Sonora.

**Built by Mr. Alex Levin in the 1870s, this was a popular public resort in Tucson and contained three acres of trees and flowers, an open-air dance hall, and a brewery. It was located at the foot of West Pennington and Pearl Street in what since became the center of Tucson's governmental building complex.

what my grandmother used to tell me—she remembered Levin's Park very well, but by the time I was born, it no longer existed.

My father's name was Nestor Córdova, and my paternal grandfather was also named Nestor Córdova. My father was born in Magdalena, Sonora, in July, 1880. He came to Tucson with his family when he was about five years old. My grandfather was a tamer of cattle, an *amanzador*. First he had to tie the cows to a *bramadero*—a large pole in the middle of the corral. Little by little they would become accustomed to being milked and then they would be tame. When he came from Mexico he was under contract with a rancher by the name of Quiroz who had a ranch on this side of the Avra Valley. He would milk cows, and then they would make cheese and they would sell the cheese.

My mother and father were married on December 21, 1901, in St. Augustine Cathedral.* When my father was first married, he went to work for Don Emilio Carrillo, who was the owner of the Las Cebadillas Ranch** in the Tanque Verde. That whole region was called the Tanque Verde because there was a water hole or tank where the cattle used to come to get water. My father was a *vaquero* (cowboy), but he also did a lot of other jobs. Afterwards, my father got a homestead on the Tanque Verde Loop Road, and that's where my sister Clara and I were raised. Since my father was not an American citizen, he could not make the claim himself, so he and Jesús Camacho, who was a policeman here, became partners, and Jesús Camacho took out the papers for the ranch.

The first house that they built there was made with *horcones* (trunks of trees with a "Y" or fork for supporting the beams) and saguaro ribs. There were nine *horcones* that supported the *vigas* or beams. The outside walls were made of saguaro ribs, and then the walls were plastered with mud. The roof was also made of saguaro ribs and mud, and saguaros were used for making walls or dividers inside the house. In 1915 we built a house and a well. The house was made of

---

*The original cathedral, built in 1862–63, was located east of the gazebo in what was to become La Placita Village in downtown Tucson. It was eventually sold and converted into a hotel and later a garage. It was razed in 1936, but its original stone facade and rose window, carved by Jules Flin, became part of the entrance to the Arizona Heritage Center on Second Street. The new cathedral on South Stone Avenue was dedicated in 1897.

**Las Cebadillas Ranch later became the world-famous Tanque Verde Guest Ranch, located at the end of Speedway on Tucson's far east side. The ranch was established by Emilio Carrillo in 1862 and remained in the Carrillo family until it was sold in 1928. Many of the original ranch buildings have been preserved, as well as the family cemetery.

adobe—it had three rooms as was the style of those days—a room for sleeping, a *sala* (living room) and a kitchen.

We had a few cattle, but mostly we farmed. We planted barley, chile, squash, watermelon, corn, tomatoes, beans, and even a little wheat. After the harvest, my father would come into town and sell the vegetables that we grew on our ranchito. My father had a wagon and a mule for coming into town. And what a mule that was! I remember that we used to have to hold the mule until my father was seated in the wagon—and then the mule would take off, and I don't think he would stop until he got into town! With the money that he made selling vegetables, my father would buy provisions. He would buy salt, sugar, wooden buckets of lard, flour, rice, kerosene, and bolts of cloth. We used the kerosene for our lamps. He would go to town about every six months, and when he returned he wouldn't think about town until the next harvest. It was an interesting life because it was very rustic, and we were so independent.

We also used to plant a few furrows of tobacco. My grandfather was in charge of the tobacco. I can remember how he was always checking on the leaves to see if they were turning yellow. As you know, the tobacco is quite a big plant—the large leaves are what are harvested. When the leaves would begin to turn yellow, he could cut them. There was a little room made out of saguaro ribs that was used for the curing. He would stack up the tobacco leaves, and he would place gunnysacks over them so that they would "sweat." After about two or three days, he would spread out the leaves so that they would dry. After the leaves would dry, he would shred the leaves, and then the tobacco would be ready. I can remember our neighbors coming from all over for some of the tobacco. Everyone rolled his own—the fine inner husks of the corn were used for cigarette paper. They would dry the husks and cut them into the appropriate lengths for cigarettes. We didn't waste anything in those days.

Although my father had the ranch, he continued to work for Don Emilio Carrillo at Las Cebadillas. When Don Emilio bought a machine for baling hay, my father was in charge of running the machine—he was the foreman. It was his job to water the horses, because of course there were no motors, and the horses ran the machine. The horses would go around and around all day, and they would drive the pistons that would push and pack the hay. There was a man who would bale the hay with a pitchfork—he was called the *taqueador*.

The Tanque Verde area was populated by many Mexican ranching families. I don't know if you have ever heard of the Aros family—Don Teófilo Aros. They had

Reflections—past and present.

a ranch above us—it was called El Mesquital. There are some descendants who are still living, but they are very old now. Their names are Don José Aros and Don Esteban Aros. Anyway, they had plenty of water on their ranch, and when they had water to spare they would come over and say, "Antonio this evening we will release some water." So the water would come down and I would irrigate our fields. When we didn't having running water my mother and I would haul water out of our well in buckets and put it in a trough to water our cattle. Abundio Otero also had a ranch close to us, and he had water rights. My mother's brother, my Tío Cristóbal Valenzuela, had a ranch on the other side of the arroyo from us. The Salcidos had a big ranch with lots of water and cattle—they were quite well to do. The Campas had a ranch across the road from the old Tanque Verde cemetery. Don Tomás Gonzales used to have a ranch up by Sabino Canyon, not too far from the ranch of Don Leopoldo Carrillo for whom Carrillo School was named. I understand that at one time the ranch belonged to Sabino Otero and that's how Sabino Canyon* got its name. Of course, all these people are gone now; the ranches were all sold. Although I still know a man who has a ranchito over on Tanque Verde Loop Road. His name is Jesús Moreno, and he is one of the oldtimers. The Mirandas lived there until recently also—Gilberto Miranda. But the old man died, and then his wife died, and who knows what has happened to the land.

One of the things that I remember best about all that ranch life were the roundups. Twice a year there were roundups. Ranchers would send their cowboys, and the foremen would direct the roundup. In those days there were no fences and the cattle wandered at will, so during the roundups the cattle would be separated according to the brand that they had. Papago cowboys would come to the roundup also. The cattle would be separated and then driven to town to sell.

We used to spend a lot of time as children up on the Sabino Canyon Ranch of Don Tomás Gonzales. My *nino* and *nina* (godfather and godmother) lived there. Their names were Ramón and Felicita Bracamonte. My *nino* was the foreman of the ranch. During the week their children would come and stay with us so that they could go to school at the old school house by the cemetery. Then, on the weekends, if there was not too much work to do at the ranch, I would go up to Sabino Canyon.

---

*Sabino Canyon was the site of much ranching activity among Mexican American settlers, later becoming part of the Coronado National Forest. Its perennial streams make it a popular recreational area. It is located at the foot of the Santa Catalina Mountains on Tucson's northeast side.

I can still remember the ranch house. It was also made of adobe and it was built in the traditional way—with three long rooms.

After my *nino* died, Ramón Quihuis became the foreman. Then after Don Tomás Gonzales sold the ranch, the new owners did not allow us to go there anymore. I never went back after that. But I am sure that the house still stands.

The first school that we attended was the one across the road from the old cemetery. It was made of adobe—it had one room, with another living area for the teachers. It had the only wooden floor in the area. I still remember the names of the teachers—Miss McDole, Miss Prim, and Miss Cotton. They couldn't speak Spanish and we couldn't speak English, so there was a little problem, but somehow we managed. Later on, when the old school house by the cemetery fell into ruin, they built a school on the other side of the Tanque Verde Wash. My uncle, Cristóbal Valenzuela, donated the land for the school.

We always managed to entertain ourselves when we were children. We would go down to the wash with our picnics and spend the whole day there playing and swimming. There was always clear running water in Tanque Verde Creek. I can also remember that when we were children we made up a game with pumpkin seeds. We would have a race to see who could peel the seeds the fastest.

Sundays were always very happy days. The families would all get together. The Galaz would come over, and the Valenzuelas and some of the other families. The guitar was very popular—everyone knew how to play the guitar. Some would play while others would dance. My father played the guitar and I played the violin. Sometimes we would dance all night. We used to play waltzes, mazurkas, polkas, and the Schottische. Sometimes we would all pitch in and send to town for an orchestra. We were very, very happy and satisfied. It was an independent life.

I remember, also, that people would sit around and tell stories. I remember sitting around and listening to the stories the cowboys told. One of the stories that they used to tell was about a train robbery in Vail. It happened that three Mexican bandits robbed the payroll train—it was called "El Pagador" because it carried the payroll for the men who worked on the railroad. In those days, gold coins were the currency. One of the bandits was captured, but not before he had buried the booty. He was sent to prison for twenty years. Then one day, on All Souls' Day, he came back to my mother's house to ask her if the Campas' house was still standing. "No," my mother said. "It fell down years ago." "Was there anything left of the house?" he asked her. "Yes," she said. "There are a few walls still standing." Then he asked her about a certain window. They continued to talk and my mother even

The adobe walls—the families—hold fast.

A hundred years—a thousand candles—a testimony of faith at El Tiradito Shrine.

gave him breakfast and then he left. Then, not long afterwards, one afternoon I hitched up a little mare to a buggy for my mother and my sister. They wanted to ride over to the cemetery to the *difuntitos* (affectionate term for the dead). That's when they saw that very same man sitting on the branch of a fallen mesquite tree. My mother stopped and asked him if he had found the house. He told her that he had found it, and that's all they said to one another. For two or three days the dogs kept barking and raising a fuss around that old ranch, but no one paid any attention to them. Then later an American named Bullcrouch went over there and found where the man had been digging. He found two or three coins that the man had overlooked. So the robber had come back—after twenty years in prison—to dig up the gold. After that there were many people who went looking for more of the treasure!

Once in a while, when the mood hits me, I go out and visit the old cemetery. My father and grandfather and grandmother are all buried there. Many of the members of the old Mexican ranching families are buried there. Many of the old graves have fallen into disrepair, and many of the graves are unmarked. But I can remember who is buried there. Some of my aunts and uncles are buried there. The Salcidos, the Bracamontes, Cruz Miranda, Juan Canelo, Feliciano Figueroa, Eulalia Figueroa, Francisca and Casimiro Ríos, and Carmela Galaz. They are all buried there in the old Tanque Verde Cemetery.

We sold the ranch in 1927 for $3,000. Can you imagine! All that land, the house, the well and the equipment, for $3,000! A lot of people sold their ranches that way. We were very poor in money, but rich in so many other ways. But we didn't know any better. The Americans would come out and offer us what seemed like a lot of money and we would take it. Then we would end up with nothing—no land, no cattle, no money. We were already rich, but we didn't know it.

Sometimes, when I am feeling sentimental, I drive out on the Tanque Verde Loop Road and drive past the old ranch house that my father and I built. It is still standing. Part of the old fence that my mother and I put up is still standing also—you can still see some of the old posts. The old adobe house has been renovated. There is a gate there now. It is called the "Linda V." A family by the name of Johnson lives there now.

HERMINIA CORDOVA
Sasabe & El Hoyo

My name is Herminia Córdova. My grandmother on my father's side of the family was from Mexico. Her name was Altagracia Espinosa de López. My maternal grandmother's name was Concepción García de López. She was from Yuma. My grandfather was Evaristo Miranda. He was from Oquitoa, Sonora, and he died very young. My father's name was Adolfo Miranda. He was born in 1880 in Oquitoa, Sonora. After his father died, he came to the United States with his mother. That was in 1885 when he was five years old. My mother and father were both raised on ranches in the Sasabe area. My father lived at Rancho de la Osa.* My mother was born on a ranch near Sasabe. It was called El Mesquital. It was not too far from Rancho de la Osa, but it doesn't exist anymore.

It was a comfortable life on the ranch. We used to watch the cowboys and the other workers. We liked to watch them milk the cows and make cheese. There were lots of little ranches all around. Refugio López lived on a little ranch. Cristolfo Arraiza lived on another. Not too far from us lived the Garcías. We used to visit one another a lot. It was also the custom to get together in the evenings to pray the rosary. We used to gather at my grandmother's house. The priest only came to Sasabe about once a month to say Mass. We used to go to Mass in horse-drawn carriages. Sometimes we would also have dances. People would come from all around—from Arivaca and Sasabe.

---

*The ranch was located about 70 miles southwest of Tucson near the Mexican border town of Sasabe, Arizona. Originally part of a 1,500,000-acre Spanish land grant to the Ortiz family, it is believed to have some of the oldest ranch structures in the state, dating from the 1700s. It later became an internationally famous guest ranch.

"There's just a little piece of El Paso Street left now."

It was hard to make it on the little ranches when there was not much land, especially when they began to fence the range. The big ranchers could make it, but the little ranchers could not, so the little ranchers began to sell off their land. My grandfather sold his ranch in 1923 and moved to another ranch close to Cocoraqui. We stayed there for a year or two and then we moved into town permanently. After we left ranching, my father went into the woodcutting business. He had a saw and he would go around to the big woodlots and cut firewood into small pieces.

I remember how I first met my husband. He and a friend came to serenade me with guitars. We were married on September 24, 1928, at St. Augustine Cathedral by Padre Pedro Timmermans. We just celebrated our fiftieth wedding anniversary. We lived in Ruby for six years after we first got married. Then we moved back to Tucson. We built our house in Barrio El Hoyo in 1941. My father-in-law bought us a lot on West Simpson. 430 West Simpson. The house still stands. My father also lived in "El Hoyo" in a little house that he built himself at 312 El Paso.

The land where the Barrio El Hoyo is located once belonged to Samaniego. Then a real estate man named Hayhurst bought it and subdivided it. Before that it had been a huge open area where they used to play baseball. Most of the people who built homes in that area were of Mexican descent. I remember so many of them. There were the Vargas and the Garcías, and Don Dolores Vásquez. Doña Virginia Gámez had a very cute house. It was blue. The Pesquieras lived on El Paso Street. And the Francos, and Manuel Miranda. Manuel Miranda was a stonemason who built the wall and pillars at the entrance to the University. He built the house at 25–33 North Westmoreland and also the stone grotto at St. Ambrose Church.

There's just a little piece of El Paso Street left now. The house that my father built was torn down. Just a small part of that old neighborhood was saved when they built that Community Center.* It's a shame. But what are you going to do? You own a little house and the city comes and says to you, "Sell us your house. If you don't sell to us, we will condemn the house." It was heartbreaking for a lot of people because they had built those houses with their own hands.

---

*In the 1960s a large segment of one of Tucson's oldest Mexican communities was condemned and bulldozed during urban renewal. In spite of community pleas to preserve the historic barrio and business area, Tucson's Community Center and parking lots were built there.

LEONARDO MARTÍNEZ
& The Rincons & Barrio Anita

My name is Leonardo Martínez. I was born in Tucson in 1906 on the corner of Sixth Street and Sixth Avenue in some apartments named the Rambaud Apartments. When my mother was expecting, my father would bring her into town from the ranch. My grandmother would go and help out until the baby was born. After the child was older, they would return to the ranch.

My father's name was Jesús María B. Martínez. The B. stands for Benítez which was the surname of his mother. My paternal grandparent's names were Juan María Martínez and Angelita Benítez de Martínez. My paternal grandparents were born in Spain. My grandmother's birthplace was either Valencia or Valladolid. And my grandfather was born in Barcelona or in that area. He was a Catalán. They were married in Spain and it was their fortune that they came to California which was the land of opportunity. In those days California belonged to Spain. I am speaking, then, about the early 19th century because my father was born in 1826 or 1827 in Sutter, California. My father was a Gachupín—a Spaniard—because his parents were born in the old country—over there in Europe, and he was born in California. Actually, my father's full name was Jesús María Benítez Martínez de la Casa de Suástique de Ureñas. That is the old style Spanish where they retain all the Spanish names.

My mother's name was Juana S. Bracamonte de Martínez. The S in her surname stood for Soto. My mother was a *cuarteña* because her father, Bracamonte, was a mestizo. That's us, *mito mita*—half and half, Spaniard and indigenous. My maternal grandmother—she must have been a beautiful woman —was pure Indian. She was a Yaqui. Her name was Serafina Soto of the Rancho de los Sotos in Sonora. That's around Imuris. My mother was a native of

Poetry and plastic at El Tiradito Shrine.

Tucson. She was born here. My mother was raised by her grandmother, Angelita. My mother's father was a wagonmaster. After he married my grandmother, Serafina, and after they had my mother, they decided to go and bring merchandise from Hermosillo. And so my mother stayed with my great-grandmother. In those days Tucson was a part of Mexico.

My father and his parents were driven out of California by the Anglos who wanted the rich land of the Sutter Valley. They fled to Hermosillo where they had family. The Duke of Alba in Spain gave a possession to the Martínez so that they could settle and establish themselves in the Valle de Hermosillo. And from the family name, Ureñas, came the name of Ures, Sonora, Mexico. There are papers to prove this. It was a land grant. This is about my ancestors. My grandparents. My father gave the *perjamino,* the parchment, to my sister. She has died, but the papers still exist. The parchment shows what was given to the family of my father's parents.

Anyway, when my grandparents and my father were fleeing from California, they passed through Tucson on the way to Hermosillo. And that is how my mother and father met. My mother told me this story: She told me that she was washing clothes in the *acequia* (spring) that is below El Tiradito.* That is where Carrillo School is now. There was a spring there where the water flowed. And that is where people washed. In those days Tucson did not exist on this side of town. The center of Tucson was over there on Meyer and Main Street—over there by El Tiradito. Anyway, she said that she saw a man coming by on a horse—a beautiful huge horse. She said that the man's hair was like gold. It was long—down his back. She saw him and he asked her, "Ma'am, will you give me a drink of water?" "Yes," my mother said. Then my father asked her where he might stay for the night and she gave him directions. The next day my father returned. "Listen, woman," he said. "Are you married?" My mother said no. "Are you a widow?" he asked. "No," said my mother. "Do you have a family?" he asked. "Yes," my mother said. "I have my grandmother here and my mother is in Imuris. But I believe she is returning soon. At least that is what Mangelita tells me." "Continue being a good woman," he said. "I will be going to Hermosillo, and when I return, I

---

*El Tiradito Wishing Shrine is a well-known Tucson historical site located on South Main near Simpson, just south of the Community Center. Its origin in the 1870s abounds with legends, but it is generally told that "El Tiradito," or little outcast, refers to a young man involved in a tragic love triangle who was killed and buried on the site. Popular belief holds that prayers said and candles lit for the soul of the dead man will help make wishes come true.

want to see you." And my mother told him, "I will wait for you." In other words, it was love at first sight. And he went away and according to my mother, it was more than a year before he returned.

My mother was a humble washerwoman. That is how she and my great-grandmother Mangelita made their living. She did not know how to read or write. But my father was very well educated. He could read and write Spanish, of course. And, you are not going to believe this—he could speak and read and write English. Also, my father could speak practically all the Indian dialects in the Southwest. He was a scout during the Indian Wars. He was known among the Indians as Chuti because they couldn't pronounce his name.

Anyway, I found out all these things when I was a boy. I was very *intruso*— intrusive—I won't deny it. That's the way you learn. Because if you don't ask a question you won't find out things. I was a *preguntón*—I asked a lot of questions.

My father was always in a good mood, and he would always answer all my questions. I remember—I must have been five or six years old—my father would put me on a big horse and we would go for a ride and he would say to me: "Look, *mihijito* (my little son), do you see that little animal over there? That animal's name is such and such. He lives in such a way. You will see him in such and such a condition and these are the places you will find him. And look! Over there! That is a bad animal. Much of the time he has rabies and you should learn to avoid him. Look, *hijo*. Do you see that weed or herb over there? The Indians say it is medicinal." And he would tell me its name. But after seventy-four years I have forgotten a lot of names. But I remember a few. And when I see a plant I tell my wife, "Look, that plant is such and such." And she asks me how I know and I answer her, "Because my father taught me."

My father returned to Tucson when he and my mother were married. My mother moved with him up to the mountains. He had homesteaded up in the Rincon Mountains, above Colossal Cave. The name of the ranch was El Ureño because, as I have said before, my father belonged to the family of the Ureñas. It was an isolated place, but my father liked it. My grandfather told him that it was like he used to see in Spain. The mountains, the trees, everything reminded him of Spain. There was a cliff and there was a spring in there. I wouldn't call it a lake, but a beautiful pond exists there. My mother used to say that there was a beautiful hickory tree—an *alizo*—in there.

The last time I was there I went with my brother, the oldest. You can get there on the old Vail Road. You have to ask permission from three different people who have land there now. Or you can go through Reddington the back way from Benson. The ranger station up there is still using some of the old buildings from my father's ranch. I know because I've been there.

My father and mother lived at the ranch for many years. They had to leave the ranch because it was made part of Coronado National Forest. When they surveyed and made the boundary the majority of what he possessed—his homestead—fell into the national forest. You see, he was a Martínez. He had a Spanish name. Next to him were the Mills and below were others. But they had Anglo names and they didn't take the land away from them. When this happened my father said, "No! This is happening again. The same thing that happened to my grandparents and parents in California. Here we go again." So he resisted. My sister had the paper and they wanted him to fight, but my father left the ranch. When the government took the ranch, they offered him money or another place, but he didn't want to have anything to do with it. They gave him, I think, $2,000 for damages. He told them that they could keep it. He tore up the papers and he burned all the evidence because they had done the same thing to his parents in California, and it was a repetition.

You know, my father used to say to me, "Son it is not a sin to desire what your neighbor has. But the greatest sin is to rob your neighbor." And I would say, "Why, father?" And he would answer, "One of these days you will know, son. Right now you do not know, but one day I will talk to you about it." And that is how I learned about what happened to my family.

Many people want facts. You have to have something to substantiate them. You have to have something that you can show to prove that these things really did happen. Then you have to go into the old records—which I have a bunch of. I have a journal where my father wrote down the business of the ranch—to whom he gave cows and from whom he received cows. There are dates and everything else. It dates to about 1864. He came to Tucson about 1851 or 1852—before the Gadsden Purchase. He was given citizenship papers because he did not want to leave to go to Mexico.

When my father left the ranch and came to town, Sam Hughes was selling lots in this area. This was known as McKinley Park, but the Mexican people who settled here renamed it Barrio Anita because the main street is Anita Street. If you notice the streets in this barrio, you notice that they are all named after pioneers—Contzen, Van Alstine, Hughes, Davis, Oury, Shilbell. Anyway, my father built the house at 826 North Anita. It belongs to my sister's estate. It is

Power to the people.

seventy years old. And he also built this house we're living in now. He built it in 1910 for my oldest sister who was getting married. There were only two rooms—the living room and the kitchen. My father knew a lot about construction. He was a woodworker and a carpenter. Both of these homes that he built are made of adobe—like the house on the ranch. If someday they knock down the house at 826 North Anita, they will find my footprints. When I was a boy I was jumping on the adobes when they were making them.

My father died in 1918 at the age of ninety-one during the Spanish flu epidemic. That left us—my mother and children—without anything. There was no other recourse but to work, so my mother returned to what she knew—that is, washing and ironing. I did whatever I could. I sold papers, magazines, flowers. I did errands. I would pick up and deliver clothes for my mother. I would take and deliver orders for enchiladas and tamales. In those days there was a big wash that ran through the barrio and in it grew parsley and different herbs. In the summer my mother would make little bunches of herbs, and I would sell them for five cents a bunch. And I would come back with a dollar or a dollar and twenty-five cents. Nowadays that doesn't seem like much, but in those days it was a lot of money.

From the time that my father died, it was very difficult. We suffered a great deal until about 1923. Then Dr. Kline and Dr. Gattell and Dr. Townsend spoke to my mother and helped her become a registered midwife. I still have her papers. And I still have the birth registrations that we used to send to Phoenix for the vital statistics. Some people still come to me to ask questions about their birth. Sometimes it's a bit sad because they think they are the child of so and so and they aren't. Sometimes, because people didn't have money, they would pay for the deliveries in trade. They would trade a chicken or whatever they had. Because she was a midwife, people thought of my mother as a doctor. They would call on her with their problems. And she would mix potions and remedies and even clean people's houses and take clean bedding when she knew that the priest was coming over with Communion.

I always wanted an education. I learned to read and write Spanish thanks to the priests here at Holy Family Church. Father Eufrasio and Father Lucas knew my father. Be aware that in those days one didn't need to speak English because 80 percent of the people in this town were Mexican and 95 percent of the people spoke Spanish. I was also an altar boy at Holy Family Church. I started out as a

Iglesia de la Sagrada Familia—a sanctuary then as now.

novitiate and became a *cardenal*. I fixed everything on the altar and when there was a pontifical mass at the church with Bishop Granjon, I was called to serve.

First I went to Davis School and then to San Agustín. My mother did not want me to go to public school. She wanted me to go to Catholic school. I also went to Santa Cruz school. When I finished grammar school, I went to Roskruge. And then I graduated from Tucson High School. Thanks to Don Santiago Ward, I was able to finish my education. He gave me a job. I would get up at four in the morning and sweep the Fourth Avenue Subway with a big broom. And then I would come home and get my books and go on to school.

Anyway, when I was older, I volunteered for the army. I was an army photographer and was sent to a special photography school in Chicago. And I have traveled. I was sent to many different places: North Africa, Iraq, Iran, Egypt. I have had a lot of different jobs in my life and I have seen a lot and learned a lot. Sometimes I think that when you are rich you don't learn as much about life. But when you are poor you have to really get out in the world and struggle and survive. And that way you learn a lot.

In the old days, it was not a stigma to be poor. Because we were all poor in this barrio and helped each other out. Before, this barrio was very pretty, very lovely, very brotherly. Everyone shared what they had because the old families were united. Most of the old families have died or gone away—Don Ignacio Caldillo's family, the Ricos, the Carrillos. And I don't know anybody now. And I don't even cross the street.

MARIA SOTO AUDELO

& The Sierritas & Barrio Histórico

My name is María Soto Audelo. I was born on July 17, 1899, in Tucson. Both my mother and my father were also born in Tucson after the Gadsden Purchase. My father, Don Ramón Soto, was born in March, 1860, and my mother, Maria Carrillo de Soto, was born in December, 1868. My mother and my father were married in the old St. Augustine Cathedral in 1886. They raised a family of three sons, Roberto, Rodolfo and Ronaldo, and one daughter. We were all baptized and married in the old St. Augustine Cathedral.

Our heritage dates back to 1774 when the Presidio was established in the walled city of Tucson. The ancestors on my father's side were descended from Captain Antonio Comadurán who came to this country from Spain. He was a captain of the old Spanish presidio of Tucson. My mother, Maria Carrillo de Soto, was the daughter of Francisco (Chico) Carrillo and Jesús (Mamachú) Córdova Carrillo. Francisco Carrillo, my grandfather, was the brother of the well-known Leopoldo Carrillo, who was a wealthy landowner and rancher. He was the owner of the famous Carrillo Gardens,* later known as the Elysian Grove.

My grandfather, Francisco Carrillo, was the founder of the famous La Sierrita Ranch. Way back in the early days, my grandfather and my grandmother were living in the vicinity of San Xavier Mission on a small *ranchito*. Here, with a few other families—the Elías and the Federícos—and with Papago Indians for neighbors, they lived quite humbly. Most of their worldly goods at that time were a

---

*Carrillo Gardens was a popular Tucson resort built by Leopoldo Carrillo in 1878. Carrillo School, on South Main, is located in the area of one of the town's first parks.

A stone corral encloses cattle—and history.

small herd of cattle and horses and poultry. But my grandfather was always thinking of more water, more range, more cattle. He had a dream of a vast domain of mountains and rolling land. With this goal in mind, he set out one day with one of his *vaqueros* (cowboys) on what was to be an exploration foray in search of a new and vast cattle frontier. When he and the vaquero had traveled many miles, they came upon that certain canyon in the Sierrita Mountains. My grandfather stopped and wanted to go no further. He was delighted with the verdure of the surrounding country and the constant flow of clear water. He made his decision right then and there. *"Aquí me clavo,"* he said. "Here is where I shall remain." It was to be the realization of a dream and the beginning of a vast domain which would one day become the heritage of my family.

But alas, there was one problem. You see, my grandfather liked to gamble. Sometimes he would win and sometimes he would lose. Sometimes there was a lot of money and sometimes not very much. It was a gambler's life. But when he would win, he would give the money to my grandmother—Mamachú we called her—so that she could count it. My grandmother was very smart. She made a little apron for my mother and it had a little pocket. She would count the money—gold and silver coins. When she would count she would tell my mother, *"Cada pilita de diez, diez a la bolsa."* "For every pile of ten coins, put ten coins in the pocket of your apron." For a rainy day. So that was their savings. When my grandfather found the land, they then had the money to buy cattle. So the credit goes to my grandmother. She was a very intelligent woman. And that was the beginning of everything. The ranch was founded in 1875 and the name of the ranch was Rancho La Sierrita. The brand was F. C., which stood for Francisco Carrillo.

When my mother and father were married, they went to the ranch, where they prospered, and my father obtained additional land. My father perfected the title of the land under the Homestead Act, and the deed was signed by President William McKinley on April 20, 1897. I still have the original deed. They built the ranch house and the rock corrals and a dam. They still stand. The dam became a landmark. It was built in 1912. It is a concrete wedge between two mountains, and it served the purpose of impounding the floodwaters. When my father was building the dam, he used to say that he was building *un monumento*. And in respect to my father, I can say that it is indeed a work of art.

In addition to being a rancher, my father was very active in community affairs. He was a very humble man and preferred to remain in the background, but there were many things that he was involved in. He was a delegate to Portland, Oregon,

"When my father was building the dam, he used to say
that he was building *un monumento*—a monument."

as a representative under Governor Brady. He was Street Commissioner in 1905 and he was instrumental in naming DeAnza Park, Paseo Redondo and Menlo Park. He gave the streets Spanish names, such as Palomas Street and Linda Street. Across from our house in town at 450 W. Congress, where the old Mulcahy Building used to be, there is a Soto Lane named after my father. It is still on the old city maps.

My father was very psychic, and he made a number of good real estate investments. We owned the building where the old Spanish language newspaper, *El Fronterizo,* was published. It was the print shop. Don Carlos Velasco was the editor. It was located at 144 West Cushing. The building still stands. And in that place was founded the Alianza Hispano Americana, on January 14, 1894. It was founded in Tucson and chapters were eventually established in 300 cities. It was founded for the mutual protection of Hispanic Americans in days of ill feeling between them and Tucson's Anglo-Saxon population. My father bought a building from Doña Pancha and transferred it to the Alianza. That is all very historic.

Anyway, my father died as a fairly young man. He died in 1922. My mom was a widow for twenty-five years. In 1933 she leased the ranch to Dan McKinney. A lot of people to this day ask me if I know the Dan McKinney Ranch. But I say, "That was never the McKinney Ranch. That was the Soto Ranch. It was just leased and never belonged to Dan McKinney."

My mother died in 1947, and my brothers and I joined in the ranching enterprise and took over the ranch again. Roberto was president, Rodolofo was vice-president, Ronaldo was treasurer and I was secretary. There were four ranches —La Cañada, La Laguna, El Tascalito, and El Rancho Grande—together with the original ranch. We had it for a number of years and then finally sold it. But our added effort carried out the dream that had originated with Don Francisco Carrillo, who one day, long ago, set out with one of his vaqueros in search of new horizons and settled, in 1875, on what is rightfully called Soto's La Sierrita Ranch.

There is a grotto at the ranch. It is close to the *pila* or watering trough and next to a natural bridge. My mother claimed that the Blessed Virgin appeared to her at the ranch many years ago. It was in the summertime. She was young and newly married and somewhat lonesome. She had just given lunch to the cowboys and she was resting—reading a *novela,* a love story. Then, all of a sudden, she turned to one side and she saw the Virgin appear at the window. My father was in another room reading the newspaper. "Ramón, Ramón!" she called. "Come here! I have just seen the Virgin! Her mantel moved." My father tried to calm my mother.

Water cooled in clay—a summer fragrance.

He tried to comfort her. But my mother believed the Virgin was trying to tell her something—that she was about to die. She used to go out to the arroyo and pray to the Virgin and ask the Virgin if she had a message. So she came to town and confessed and the priest told her that even if it was a dream, nevertheless, it was a beautiful one.

We always knew the story of my mother and the Virgin, and so, after many, many years had passed, we bought her a statue of *La Virgen Milagrosa* and built the grotto. And the grotto is still there, and the statue of the Virgin is still there. Many people have come and gone, but the Virgin remains. She is looking after the ranch; she is protecting it. It is as if the Virgin were saying, "I belong here. And you must let me stay."

My brothers lived on the ranch with my father. When my brothers were small, my mother taught them the alphabet and the *doctrina* (catechism). I was already twelve years old the first time I visited the ranch. My mother and I lived in town in our town house. Our house in town was located at 126–130 West Cushing Street. It was a beautiful barrio. Across the street from us lived Genaro Manzo and his lovely family. Next to us lived Mr. Montijo. The house still stands. Then the Urías. It was beautiful in the morning. Mr. Urías used to play the flute and his daughter would play the piano. I would practice the piano early in the morning. I had a beautiful piano. And Mr. Manzo would play the cornet. Mr. Montijo, on our side of the street, used to play the violin. And his daughter Lolita would sing. One of Mr. Montijo's sons was also a violinist. It was beautiful. We were all one. No one thought himself better than anyone else. Everyone respected everyone else. Early on Sunday mornings, Don Quirino would come with a little red wagon with a huge fifty gallon can of *menudo* (tripe soup). He would call out, "Menudo! Menudo!" And everyone would come out and buy menudo. How we all enjoyed those things.

I have a lot of happy memories. I remember that on the Fourth of July in 1917, when I was still a young girl, Don Francisco Moreno* and Don Carlos Jácome** came to ask my father permission for me to represent Mexico in the *Carro*

---

*Don Francisco Moreno was the publisher of *El Tucsonense,* a Spanish language newspaper published in Tucson from 1914–1959.

**Don Carlos Jácome was a prominent pioneer businessman who came to Tucson from Sonora in 1866. The family department store which he founded remained in business in downtown Tucson until 1980.

The Virgin Mary keeps a vigil at La Sierrita Ranch.

Alegórico, a float. They came in person. My father said to check with my mother, and my mother said that it was all right with her if it was all right with me. So I accepted. My mother made my dress. It was embroidered with sequins.

I remember, also, when the circus would come to town. My mother used to rent the land to the circus. It is where the Desert Inn is now. We always got choice seats and free tickets for the rides because my mother owned the land.

And I don't want to forget to tell you about the Teatro del Carmen. My father's sister, Carmen Soto Vásquez, built the Teatro. The building still stands —it is on South Meyer and is now the black Elk's Club. It was very famous. There were musicals and dramas and operas. Very famous actors came, Adolfo Gutiérrez and his wife and Armando Calvo. They were in the category of the Barrymores. The Teatro del Carmen was a Spanish-speaking theatre and the artists came from Mexico. People always looked forward to going. It was a beautiful and elegant affair.

We are very proud to be part of these lovely memories.

ALBERTO S. URIAS

& Barrio Libre & Carrillo Gardens

My name is Alberto Salazar Urías. I was born in Tucson on July 4, 1904, on Cushing Street. My father's name was Francisco Urías, and my mother's name was Ambrosia Salazar Urías. My grandfather, Juan Urías, was born in 1817 in what was called Barrio San José, near the old Mission of San Cosme* which was located at the foot of "A" Mountain. He used to have land along the Santa Cruz River—he was a farmer. My grandfather also owned six sections of land where Casas Adobes is now. He homesteaded it. He had a little adobe house right there on the way to Florence. A man named Waters took possession of his land, because in the old days the people did not have land titles. So the judge decided in the American's favor, and my grandfather lost all his land.

There were a lot of Mexican people who had ranches in those days—many of them lost the rights to their land. The Palafox, the Valenzuelas, the Garcías, the Vacanoras, the Rodríguez—they all had ranches. The Vacanoras had a ranch right where the Animal Shelter is now. Many of them lost their lands in the courts. One of the few who survived were the Ronstadts—they still have a ranch, the Santa Margarita, over by the Baboquívari Mountains.**

Nothing remains of the Barrio San José and the Mission of San Cosme. The old Mission of San Cosme was built by the Spaniards about the same time that San

---

*The old mission of San Cosme is thought to have been built by Franciscan missionaries at the end of the eighteenth century. The old ruins of the historic church and school west of the Santa Cruz River could still be seen in the early 1900s, but today no traces remain.

**The Ronstadt family no longer owns the Santa Margarita Ranch. The family hardware business, founded by the Ronstadt brothers in 1898, was still in operation on Sixth Avenue and East Pennington in downtown Tucson in the early 1980s.

The leaves of the cottonwoods rustle—or is it the laughter of children playing?

Xavier was built. The church was made of adobes and the convent for the sisters was made of stone. My grandfather used to tell me that there was a tunnel going from the church to "A" Mountain. It was called Sentinel Peak in the old days, because that's where a sentinel was posted to watch for Apache attacks. When the Apaches were coming, the watchman would come down the tunnel from the top of the mountain and run into town to warn the people.

Once, when I was about fourteen years old, I was over there at the old church. You could still see the walls then. I noticed in the adobe wall that there was a patch about 7 feet tall by 2 feet wide. I began to dig, and that's when I found a skeleton in the wall—who knows how old the skeleton was. I told the authorities, but they never did anything about it.

When I was a child, there was a tribe of Apache Indians that lived in an encampment right at the foot of "A" Mountain. It's where the Holiday Inn is now. There used to be a well right here where we live now, and the Indians used to come and get water from the well. It was sweet water. We had a little table outside, like we do now, and they always used to leave a little token on the table—a bowl of pinole, beef jerky, corn tortillas. They never spoke, except to my grandmother, because she could speak the Apache language.

The Santa Cruz had water all year round. The water ran clear, about eighteen to twenty inches deep. All along the river there were groves of willows and huge cottonwoods. The trees were so lush that they arched over the river. People would go and hunt and fish along the river—there was everything aplenty. There were ducks and quail and doves and rabbits—and even fish. There were large rocks along the river and the women would go down to wash and gossip along the river. It was a sight to behold. They would make soap from a plant named *amole*. They would crush the fibers of the plant with a rock. When they finished washing, they would spread the clothes to dry over the bushes along the river—the clothes looked like flowers on all the bushes. Then they would wash their long, beautiful hair.

*El Día de San Juan** was a favorite feast day of the Mexican people. Early in the morning they would go down and bathe in the river. There was a lot of food

---

*San Juan's Day, commemorating the birth of St. John the Baptist, was a popular fiesta in early Tucson history. Dancing, racing, picnicking, and swimming in the Santa Cruz River marked the festivities. Tradition taught that it aways rained on the 24th of June.

and music. Everywhere you could hear the sound of guitars. There were horse races also—they used to race over where St. Mary's Hospital is now. They used to play a game called "El Gallo." It was kind of a rough game. The cowboys would bury a rooster up to his neck in the dirt, and then they would try to grab the rooster while riding full speed on horseback.

Right here, next to where I live now, was the Carrillo Gardens. It was beautiful—about eight acres of trees and flowers. There were all different kinds of roses from throughout the world. There were huge cottonwood trees, and even a little zoo. There was also a small lake and a little kiosk. There was a little boat, and the musicians would ride in the little boat and serenade the people. They would play all day Saturday and Sunday. The trolley car—it was pulled by mules—would leave the people right here at the garden on the corner of Main and Simpson. There was also a pavilion where there was dancing and skating. Carrillo Gardens was owned by Leopoldo Carrillo—he was a wealthy rancher. It seemed as if every day there was a fiesta. We used to celebrate the patriotic holidays here—the Fourth of July and the Sixteenth of September, which is Mexican Independence Day. For the big fiestas the ranchers from all the surrounding area would bring in whole beef, and they would barbecue them right here. You can still see the traces of the pits that they dug for the barbecue.

I know that there is a legend about the Carrillo Gardens. People say that the devil appeared at the dancing pavilion one night. But I know that the story is not true, because I was there. It happened about 1916. This fellow named Churri Ríos—he lived over on the corner of Eighteenth—he was a practical joker. Well, one night, he made a rooster foot for himself, and dressed up all in black. He wore a long black coat and a black tie and he made a long black tail which he attached to his coat. He was dancing when someone noticed his rooster foot. Everyone started to scream, "The Devil! The Devil!" Everyone ran away and people were frightened and stopped coming to the Gardens. There were no more dances and they eventually closed the Gardens. That's how the legend of the Devil in the Carrillo Gardens got started.*

---

*The folktale of the appearance of the devil with the claw of a rooster and the hoof of a goat is a classic Mexican legend which dates back to colonial times. It is told, with local variations, throughout Mexico and the Southwest, and often deals with the theme of a disobedient daughter.

I know another story—the story of El Tejano.** I know that story because my father was deputy sheriff of Tucson. He was a young man when this happened. The stagecoach route came from Gila Bend and went around the back way to El Cerro del Gato. The old road is still there. The stagecoach used to carry the payroll of the miners and ranchers, gold and silver coins. El Tejano used to rob the stagecoach, but he was very clever and they could never catch him. There was an old blacksmith shop on Simpson and Main—the blacksmith's name was Don Cayetano. El Tejano used to take his horse there to be shod, but he would make them put the horseshoes on backwards so that when they tried to follow his trail they always went the wrong way. Well, he was finally betrayed by someone, and the posse lay in wait for him one day when he was about to rob the stagecoach. It was early in the morning, and they captured and killed him right there where Silverlake used to be. But no one could ever figure out what he had done with all his booty. I know a lot of people who have gone up to look for the Tejano's treasure up on El Cerro del Gato, but no one has ever found it. Some people say that the ghost of El Tejano will appear if you go and look for his treasure, but I don't believe that—I think it is just the noise of the dust devils.

Well, everything is different now. Over there where the Community Center is was a beautiful Mexican neighborhood with many grand and beautiful houses. They have all been torn down, and many of the Mexican families have died off or moved away. I have an old city directory from the 1930s, and of all the old families, there are only two remaining—us and the Palafox. Yes, those were good times, and I have a lot of memories, but all that has changed.

**The legend of El Tejano, or The Texan, was a popular story in Tucson at the turn of the century. It is said to be based on the life of a minor outlaw named William Brazelton. Oral tradition has embellished the story. El Tejano was said to have been a latter-day Robin Hood who robbed from the rich and gave to the poor. Popular lore holds that his treasure is hidden on Cat Back Mountain—El Cerro del Gato—which is located west of Kennedy Park just off the Ajo Highway. The ghost of El Tejano riding his horse is said to be protecting the cache, and many sightings of the specter have been reported over the years.

ELINA LAOS SAYRE
The Old Pueblo

My name is Elina Sayre. My mother's name was Teresa Laos Sayre. It's a big Tucson family. My mother's family came originally from Spain and they settled in Hermosillo, Sonora, Mexico. My grandmother's name was Carmen Laos and my grandfather's name was Fernando Laos. The family came to Tucson when the French invaded Mexico; my grandfather had died by that time. The French came in on horseback, and they were stealing all the young girls, so my grandmother left Hermosillo immediately and came to Nogales by stage. There were no trains then. Fortunately, they had some very good friends in Nogales—Don Ramón and his family—and they stayed with them for a while. Then, when the first train came to Nogales, my grandmother brought her daughters to Tucson by train. Tucson was naturally a small town at that time, but there were many beautiful pioneer families. When they came here, my mother became acquainted with Mrs. Sam Hughes—Atanacia Hughes. Atanacia loved my mother, so she said to her, "Teresita, I have just the right man for you." His name was William Aron Sayre. He was a widower. His parents were from New England, and my father was born in Newark, New Jersey. My father and mother were married in the old St. Augustine Cathedral where the Placita is now. My father was an engineer. He worked for the ice company that was down on Twelfth Street and then later he worked for the railroad.

I remember the old Cathedral—naturally I must have been very young when I saw it. But when I was a child we lived very close to it. We lived on West Camp Street—that's where Broadway is now. In the old days it wasn't Broadway. And the reason they called it Camp Street is because at the end of the street there was a camp of soldiers.

I was born in Tucson at our home at the corner of Scott and Camp Street on September 16, 1889 at five o'clock in the morning. The 16th of September is Mexican Independence Day. The Philharmonic Band was going by our house in a parade celebrating Independence Day. I used to tell my mother that they were celebrating my birthday! We rented the house on Camp Street—there was a row of adobe houses—from a French family who lived here in Tucson. Their name was Charouleau.

Then we lived on Convent Street for a while. It was still the horse and buggy days. In the summertime, people would sleep outside, and my father had a cot made for each one of us. No one was afraid of robbers then; we were just as happy and secure as God is in Heaven. Every morning we would put our cots up against the wall and that's how we would make our beds.

There were no markets then. My mother used to buy lard in little five pound cans, and when she finished with the lard, she would save the cans. Every night, she would hang the little pails on a nail on the door, and the milkman would come and fill the little pails with milk. And all the doors of the houses of those days had transoms. And later on in the day the baker would come and leave the loaves of bread on the transoms. And later on in the day the Chinaman would come with his horse and wagon—the wagon was full of all kinds of clean and beautiful vegetables. And my mother would select fresh vegetables from his wagon every day. And all of us children would wait by the vegetable wagon and he would give us carrots or a piece of sugar cane. And we would dance around the wagon as happy as could be.

The Chinese people had farms all along the Santa Cruz River. That's where they raised their vegetables and where we had picnics. It was very beautiful—there was lots of water and many trees. We would lay our picnic out right along the banks of the river. We would play the guitar and sing. My mother used to play the guitar beautifully and she had a beautiful soprano voice. We knew the owner of the farm and he would come and have dinner with us and he would bring us a big sweet watermelon. Oh, we used to have so much fun! We had a picnic of one kind or another almost every Sunday.

San Juan Day, the 24th of June, was a big day on the river. It was always a big fiesta because there were so many Juans and Juanitas. There were many serenades.

All of Convent Street was a beautiful neighborhood. Right next to us lived the Hughes family. And then next to them lived Al Buehman—he was the only photographer in Tucson. Across the street from us lived Luz Villaescusa. She was my *nina* (godmother) of my confirmation. It's all gone now, of course. They knocked down all those beautiful old homes.

Later on we lived at 32 West Corral. We rented our home there also. The houses were regular adobe and they had patios. In the afternoons we would go out and water our front yards and the sidewalks. There were no real sidewalks then, of course. It was all dirt. Every evening after supper we would take our chairs and sit out in front of the house. Mama and Papa would visit with the neighbors, and we would play hopscotch and jump-rope. While we would be sitting out in the evening in the cool air, we would hear a sound. Clop, Clop, Clop. And who was it but the policeman, Jesús Camacho, on horseback. And he knew everybody. And he would greet everybody, "hello here" and "hello there."

Every Sunday when we would leave the house to go to church, there would be a beautiful bouquet of flowers tied to the knob of the door. I was about eighteen and I was singing in the cathedral at the time. We would go up in the choir loft and sing the Mass. Mr. Antonio Coenen was the organist and Mr. Carlos Jácome and I would sing. I would sing the Ave María. I remember when they renovated the cathedral on Stone. Everybody was sorry about that because we loved that old church.

When I was a young girl we would go to the Placita where the first St. Augustine Cathedral was. There was a gazebo in the center of the plaza and a string orchestra played there. The gazebo was so beautiful. It was very ornate. It had a roof over it and it had pillars and all around there was interlaced woodwork. And it had steps going up to it. There was grass all around it and great big boulders that we used to sit on. We would sit on the boulders or on the grass and listen to the orchestra. At that time there were no trumpets or cornets. The orchestra was a string orchestra, as I have said, with violins, guitars and violas. When the boys came we would get up and parade on the inside circle around the gazebo. And the boys would make another circle and parade on the outside in the opposite direction. And then the first thing you knew, the boys would be intermingling with the girls. We would be all dressed up with long beautiful dresses and we wore hats with feathers or flowers. Everything was handmade in those days. There was no ready-to-wear. My mother was a beautiful seamstress. We even made our own hats.

Sometimes on Sunday we would go for a *barbacoa* to the Amado Ranch* out

*See Chapter 13.

"Sometimes on Sunday we would go for a *barbacoa* . . . in a wagon pulled by four horses."

on the Nogales Highway. We would all go in a wagon pulled by four horses. We would hire an orchestra—the Montijo Orchestra. It was made up of members of one family. Before we got to the ranch we could smell the wonderful aroma of the barbecue cooking. They used to dig a big pit to cook the meat in. There was a long table with a white cloth. There was always so much food. Big pots of beans and green chile salsa and corn and stacks and stacks of tortillas. And then we would dance. The girls all wore long beautiful dresses. We would dance waltzes and mazurkas.

I worked for fifty-one years of my life. I worked for Mr. Jácome and Mr. Manzo at their first store at 90 West Congress. It was called La Bonanza. I worked for Mr. Jácome for 28 years and for Mr. Myerson for 23 years. First I worked at Mr. Jácome's West Congress Street store and later at the East Congress Street store.

Those were beautiful, romantic days. I have a lot of beautiful memories and that's why I say that I would like to go back and relive those days. They were full of happiness, love, music and *abrazos* (embraces). We all loved one another and helped one another the best we could. Sometimes, you see, when I am alone in this room and when I get tired of watching TV or reading, I just go to bed and reminisce. I have had a wonderful life. I am very lucky.

JACINTA CARRANZA
& Fort Lowell & Barrio Anita

My name is Jacinta Jacobo Carranza. I was born on January 28, 1902, in an old adobe where Ft. Lowell Park* is now. The house that I was born in no longer exists—all the houses were torn down when that area was made into a park.

My father's name was Jesús Jacobo. He came as a very young man from Sinaloa, Mexico. My mother's name was Angelita Pereira de Jacobo. My mother was born in Arizona in an area called San Pedro. It is over there on the other side of the big mountain range where the San Pedro River is. My maternal grandparents were also born in the San Pedro area—they were farmers.

My father was a farmer also. In the olden days, all that land where Ft. Lowell Park is now—and all along the Rillito River—was all farm land. There were many Mexican families who lived there in those times, and they were all farmers.** When the soldiers were moved from Ft. Lowell, the walls of the buildings were left standing. They removed everything made of wood—the windows and doors. And then the poor people put roofs on the abandoned buildings and they added windows and doors. We fixed them up as best we could so that we might live there. It was all abandoned and one didn't have to ask permission. We lived close to the river; the Pantano and the creek from Sabino joined there at the park and there was a lot

---

*Located at Fort Lowell Road and Swan Road, Fort Lowell Park was once the site of an army post. The post was moved to New Mexico in 1891 and army property and materials were sold at a public auction. The commanding officer's quarters, now renovated, was a branch museum of the Arizona Heritage Center in the early 1980s.

**The Mexican settlement or *ranchería* which grew up in the abandoned buildings of the old fort was known as "El Fuerte." It was an agricultural community and many of the residents of the Ft. Lowell Historical Neighborhood trace their roots to that original settlement.

"There are still little crosses where you can see the names of my people."

of water. There were also many trees—cottonwoods, willows and *tápiros.* We used to play there.

My father planted a lot of corn, squash, watermelon, beans and all other kinds of vegetables. He would harvest his crops and then he would come to town to sell his vegetables. He would sell the produce to the markets in town. Sometimes my father would bring us all to town when he came to sell so that we could buy shoes and clothes and whatever else we might need. We came to town in a little horse-drawn cart. I remember those little carts very well. In those days Congress Street was full of stores. We used to go to the store of Don Carlos Jácome. He was the father of Alejandro Jácome, Sr. The name of their store was La Bonanza.

It was a good life—we didn't lack anything. We grew everything we needed in our *milpita,* and what we didn't grow we would buy with the money from our crops—staples like lard, meat, coffee and flour.

As I said, there used to be a lot of Mexican families there, but most of them have died, and the others have moved away and have scattered. There are a few Mexican families who still live there in the Ft. Lowell area, but now many of the old adobe houses are owned by Anglos. There were several families by the name of Díaz who lived there. My sister's father-in-law's name was Jorge Díaz—he was from Sonora—and I think some of his family might still live there. Then there was Bernardino Díaz—he was not related. But that family does not exist anymore—neither the parents nor the children—they have all died. There was a family by the name of Soto and another family by the name of Ochoa. And there were the Olivas who were relatives of the Ochoas.

There were also some Mormon families who were living in the area farther down the river. They had dairy cattle. There is an old cemetery where the Catholic Mexican families buried their dead. The Mexican cemetery is on Ft. Lowell as you go around that big bend. It is right there on the very corner. All my family is buried there—my mother and my father, my brothers and my sisters, and nieces and nephews. There are still little crosses there where you can see the names of the people—my father and mother's names are still there. I used to go there with my daughters on November 2, All Souls Day, and we used to take flowers to all the *dolientes* (suffering souls). But now I cannot go anymore because I am too sick. But I know that a lot of Mexican people still go there on All Soul's Day to put wreaths of flowers on the graves.

We used to have our own little church in that barrio. The first church that we had there—it was really just a little chapel—was called San Angel de la Guardia. It

Remnants of the desert and devotion.

was right there on Ft. Lowell Park where we had our houses, but a windstorm knocked it down. Then another little church was built, and that chapel was called San Pedro. It was on some land that was owned by a woman named Doña Josefa Mulé. Her husband's name was Don Ignacio Mulé. They had forty acres of land, and they built a church right next to their house. Once a month the fathers would come from town to say Mass. The people always knew when the fathers would be coming and they would all gather at the chapel. That little church of San Pedro still exists. You can see it from Ft. Lowell Road. It is a residence now and someone actually lives in it. I believe they are Americanos. I am not sure if the little belltower where the little bell was still exists.*

The people were very religious—they venerated different saints, and every house had its own special saint. On Christmas Eve, the people would get together and venerate the Holy Child. And on March 19th, they would venerate St. Joseph. They would get together and pray and sing.

But the fiesta that I remember best was the Fiesta of San Isidro. He was venerated by everyone because he is the patron saint of farmers. On St. Isidro's Day, May 15th, all of the farmers in the area where we lived made a procession through the *milpas* (fields). They made the procession praying and singing praise so that God and San Isidro would help them—that the year's planting might be successful so that they might have crops to sell. And they prayed to San Isidro so that they might have enough rain for their crops. Two men would carry the statue of San Isidro on a little table on their shoulders. The statue would be decorated with flowers. Then, during the procession, they would make little offerings from each milpa—a little bunch of onions, an ear of corn, some squash. They would put these offerings to San Isidro on the little table, being careful all the while that the little statue did not fall off. It was very interesting and very charming, and the people were very contented as they walked along praying and singing. And I guess that San Isidro was contented also, because he always answered our prayers and we always had a good harvest.

My husband's family was from Sonora. My husband's name was Simón Salazar Carranza. He worked in the mines in Miami and Superior. He also worked in California for a while. He became good friends with one of my brothers who loved to play the guitar and sing. And that's how I met my husband. We fell in love.

*The San Pedro Chapel was dedicated in January, 1982, as an historic site and as of that date was no longer a residence.

"Some saladitos, a loaf of bread and a can of milk, *por favor.*"

We were married in 1924. When we were first married we stayed at Ft. Lowell, and he became a farmer also. After ten years, he decided to work for the railroad, and that's when we moved to town. He worked in the Roundtower (*La Redonda*) cleaning and repairing machinery. He bought the lot here in Barrio Anita, and we lived in a little house out back while we were waiting for him to build this house. It took us a long time to finish the house—there was a shortage of building materials during the war.

I have never worked outside the home. My husband didn't want me to work—he said it wasn't necessary. He said that he supported me so that I could care for the children. And that is how I have spent my life—caring for my children. Even after my husband died in 1953, I did not leave the house to work. I worked right here—washing, ironing, cooking—and my children went to work to help out. I always loved my children very much—I never wanted to be apart from them because I worried that something might happen to them. They were always at my side. I didn't like for them to spend too much time at other people's houses— I didn't like them to be bothering other people. So I taught my daughters how to embroider, and I kept my sons busy sweeping and raking up the yard.

I used to be able to walk to church to go to Mass. Holy Family Church is very close—just across the railroad tracks. But now I am not well and cannot walk there anymore, so Father comes every Friday to give me Communion. When my children were little I always used to tell them that they could not go to the movies if they did not go to Mass. So they would take their baths and get dressed and go to Mass and then I would let them go to the movies. I have always been religious and have had a lot of faith. I am especially devoted to the Virgen de Guadalupe,* and she has been good to me and taken care of me and my children and protected us from harm. I prayed to her while my sons were in the Korean War and she brought them home safely.

We moved to Barrio Anita in 1933—I have lived here for almost fifty years. When we moved here, we already had five children, but three of my children— Connie, Simon and Carmen—were born in this house. I used to know a lot of people in this barrio, but most of them have died or gone away. I remember Don

---

*The Virgin of Guadalupe, the patron saint of the Americas, is said to have appeared to an Indian named Juan Diego on Tepeyac Hill near Mexico City, in 1531. She is the object of much veneration among persons of Mexican descent who consider her their protectoress. Her feast day, December 12, is of great religious importance.

La Virgen and the V-8—Barrio Anita.

Francisco Cruz and his wife, Doña Virginia. And Fedicio and María Campas and Juan and Manuelita Aguirre and Doña Jesús (Chui) Goday. I remember the Carrillos—Don Féderico and Doña Guadalupe. Our children all used to play together. And the García family—their son still lives here—his name is Frutoso García. And Mr. and Mrs. Roxie Moore still live here. And Sra. Monica Ballesteros has lived here for a long time. She lives in that little house behind me and often comes to visit me. Anyway, most of the old families are gone—some of the old houses have been torn down. People used to stay in one place in the old days, but now they move around a lot. Many of the people who live in this barrio now rent the houses, and I hardly know anyone anymore.

HENRY GARCIA

& El Hoyo The Old Pueblo

My name is Henry García. This is what I remember of the genealogy of my family. First of all, my mother was born in Tucson in about 1894. Her name was Guadalupe Rubalcava. She was born in an old barrio by what is now the Fourth Avenue subway. It was called *El Tiburón* (The Shark) or *La Isla de Cuba* (The Island of Cuba) because of the big arroyo that ran through that area. It was bordered by Fourth Avenue and Ninth Street—ask any old-timer—he will tell you about it. You can still see parts of the big arroyo now. In fact, my grandmother drowned in that wash in a big flood. After she died my grandfather returned to Hermosillo because he had some property there. That is where my father and mother met and were eventually married.

My father's name was Margarito García. He was born in the state of Guanajuato, Mexico, and came to the United States in about 1905. He was a tailor and for a time he worked for Capins who were located in Tucson before they moved to Nogales. For a time he returned to Mexico and after he married he returned again to Tucson. My parents then opened a little tailor shop on Congress Street—West Congress. My father made custom clothes. Later he moved his business to South Meyer. It was a tailor and drycleaning establishment and its name was Garden City Cleaners.

All of us were born here except for my oldest sister, who was born in Hermosillo. I was born on Meyer Street in 1921. We lived on Meyer Street in an area that was called El Corral. At first we had our home right where our business was, but in 1923 my parents built a house in the barrio called El Hoyo. Our house was built of adobe, of course. My father had the house built by a contractor called El Chapulín. I can't remember his real name—only his nickname. When we first built our house we drew our water from a well and used kerosene lamps for illumination. I remember that my mother used to say that the adobes in our house were not mortared with mud, but with *mezcla*—that is, cement and lime mortar.

Our house was at 218 El Paso Street—there is still a little piece left of El Paso Street, but where our house used to be is now part of the parking lot of the Community Center. Urban Renewal also tore down our old store on South Meyer—it has been gone for some time now. My brother has continued in the drycleaning business, however; it's called García's Cleaners and it is now located on 22nd Street and 5th Avenue. He has a lovely place of business, but as for me, I got out of the business. I work for the state now.

Now that I remember, the life in those old barrios was a full and rich one. We all lived together—there was a mixture of people—Jews, Syrians, naturally many Mexicans, Chinese, Lebanese—and everyone spoke Spanish.

You know, when I think about my memories as a boy, the life of a child today seems sterile in comparison. *Sin chiste*—without flavor. Everything children of today know, they get from the TV. It seems to me that they know very little of real life. It's sad, because everything is so spread out and disconnected now—there's no sense of community. People stay inside their houses. They don't seem to want to live close to anyone. It's as if people hate one another. Everyone wants to live on an acre—no one wants to have neighbors.

Anyway, as I have said, in those days we all lived close together—one house was right next to the other and women visited over the fence. A boy could have a lot of adventures. I saw a lot of things and learned a lot.

I remember that in front of us lived a gentleman by the name of Dolores Vásquez. He made adobes for a living. You know, I know how to make adobes because as a child, I spent a lot of time watching him. He had a wagon and two horses and he used to bring the dirt from nearby—I'm not exactly sure where he got the dirt, possibly from the Santa Cruz River. He would make the adobes right there in his yard and then he would deliver them.

Then right next to us lived the Miranda family. The father was a woodcutter. He had a machine that had a gasoline engine. It had wheels and he would haul it from house to house with a truck. He would cut wood at the homes and that is how he earned his living.

On the other side of us lived a carpenter. He made cabinets out of wood. He made little tables and chairs and cupboards for children. I would sit and watch him. And a little farther on there was a man who was a *talabartero*. I remember sitting and watching him make saddles and boots. He would decorate the leather objects with beautiful designs. He made harnesses and belts also and all kinds of leather things. His name was Palemón Díaz. And then a little farther down lived Guillermo García of La Suprema Tortilla Factory. Then there were the López and the Borboas. Then there were the Trujillos—they were a very big family and many of them still live in the Tucson area.

Another person that I remember was Don Benito. He was a kind of "character" living in El Hoyo. He was a hunchback—a little old man. He made his living cutting and splitting wood with an axe. He would charge four *reales* or six *reales* to split wood. He was also a *brujo* (sorcerer) or *curandero* (traditional curer). He sold potions. He would give you a potion, for example, if you had fallen for a certain girl. He would give it to you and you would wear it around your neck in a little red pouch. I don't know if the potions worked, but maybe they worked because they would give you confidence.

As I was saying—it was a beautiful life. There were a lot of fiestas. Anytime there was a baptism or birthday there was a fiesta. There was always music—the music of Goyo Esquer, the music of the Orquesta Corral. The fiestas and dances were held in the yards of the houses. They would water down the patios and put up strings of lights. Then the musicians would arrive and the people of the barrio would come together.

And I don't want to forget to tell you about the Teatro del Carmen. My mother used to tell me about it. That's where all the Mexican society used to go. They would go out to the functions in the evening all dressed up and elegant. Mr. Otero would go to the theatre all elegant. Performers came from Mexico—famous people like the Hermanos Soler, Virginia Fábricas and Esperanza Iris. The Teatro del Carmen still exists—did you know that? It is now the black Elks Club on South Meyer. I was there not too long ago—I guess it's been eight or ten years now. I peeked to see what was what. And do you know that the part of the old *teatro* where the stage was still exists! Then there was the Teatro Royal. It was located where the south parking lot of the Community Center is now. It was a brick building with towers in the front. Musicians would play there, and there was also Mexican vaudeville. They also had puppet shows there and later, films.

As I was saying, I really used to get around as a boy. My father would send me on errands and I would deliver trousers that had been cleaned and pressed. I would get to see a lot of places making those deliveries for my father. I used to go see Miguel Díaz. He was a blacksmith who had a shop in Elías' stable. Díaz' place

Paradise lost—Barrio El Hoyo.

was like an old-fashioned blacksmith shop. He had an old-fashioned forge. He made wheels and he would also repair things. Elías' stable was on Main Street. I believe that is also where the Community Center parking lot is now. He used to board horses there. When the Papagos would come to town to sell wood or to buy supplies, they would feed and water their horses at Elías' stable. I remember that Elías had a very pretty mare and a very pretty buggy. Every evening he would go out and ride around in his buggy. His mare was very proud and would prance with her tail up.

Then there was the hardware store owned by Mr. Villaescusa—it was on Meyer Street. It was a first class hardware store. You know that full-sized plaster horse in front of Porter's western wear store? Well, it used to be in front of Villaescusa's hardware store. Joaquin Carrillo also had a hardware store, and there were other drycleaning establishments there on Meyer besides that of my father. One belonged to Señor Aquiles Rodriquez and another to Señor Faustino Perez.

There were four bakeries that I remember—there was the Panadería de Don Juan on Broadway next to Palemón Díaz, the leatherworker. Then there was the Panadería Internacional—it belonged to a man named Miltenberg. Then there was the Panadería La Guaymense that belonged to Pancho Trujillo. We used to go into the bakeries—you know how little boys are into everything. They used to let us go in and watch them make bread. Now everything is regulated—it's against the law—that's what everything says. They're afraid that there might be an accident and someone might get sued. Everyone lives with so much caution and fear—we have lost a lot of liberty because of it.

As I was saying, we used to go and watch them work at the bakeries. They had the ovens outside. I remember best the *panadería* of Don Panchito. Up until they demolished to make way for the Community Center, the oven that he used was still in existence. He was an old man with a big moustache, and he walked kind of hunched over and crooked. His specialty was a pastry called *fruta del horno*— fruit of the oven. He would come from Simpson to Congress with a little table and he would sell his little pastries to people who were going to the movies at the Plaza and the Lyric. And he would pay my brother and his friends to carry the little table to Congress Street and then back home again.

Speaking of those old days, and how things have changed, here is a favorite story of mine. I call this story The Lamplighter of Tucson. Over there in La Placita there used to be a little house made out of brick. And inside there were a lot of switches, controls and panels that were for turning on the lights of Tucson. When it began to get dark, a man would come with a great many keys. He would open the doors and turn on the switches, and the lights would go on in the town. Then he would go walking along a certain route—he must have covered a lot of territory—and he would check all the lights. He had a little notebook and he would make a note wherever there was a light bulb that had gone out in a street lamp— that way it could be replaced the next day. And he went on foot all along Stone and Sixth and Broadway and Main. Then in the early morning he would come and open up the door of the little house and he would turn off all the switches. And then he would go to the Tucson Electric Power Company—that's where Jácome's Department Store is now—and he would take his report. It's hard to believe that one man would go and turn on the lights of Tucson.

I could tell you a lot more about those old days and the businesses and the people and the families—families that used to live in El Hoyo who have now all gone away and scattered. I can tell you how the people in that area did without for so many years. At first we did without running water, and then a water main was put in. Then we did without electricity, and they finally put in lights. And for so many years, the streets were not paved. In the old days that area was also known as Barrio El Sapo because when it rained (the earth in that area was very black and rich—it used to be farmland) big frogs used to come out and they would sing all night long. You could hear the frogs all the way to Congress Street. When it rained it got so muddy that cars couldn't go in without getting stuck—they used to have to leave the cars up on Main Street. I remember once that the milkman got stuck in the mud and was stuck all night long.

Anyway, as I was saying, after so many years of doing without water and electricity, after all the houses were paid for and modernized and made more comfortable, after all the little gardens were flourishing—that's when the City decided to take the homes away from the people and evict them. They were all old people who had lived there for many years and who had never moved. And it was a very difficult time for everyone. And what good did it do to fight? In those days the only thing the City thought about was to demolish, demolish, demolish. It was a stupidity, an idiocy, a barbarity. You know, I have traveled around—I have been to New Orleans, to Santa Fe, Boston—I have seen what has been done with the old houses in those cities. If the City had had the sense to leave some of those old homes, they could have been renovated and preserved and people would have been interested in them and gone to see them. But the way it is now—the Community Center—no one goes there, not even the flies. Have you noticed? It is practically abandoned most of the time. And all those new stores that they made in La

Placita Village—no one goes there. Why? Because they knocked down all those old houses and stores and then they built new ones. It's all fake and people don't go there because they don't like the artificial. They like genuine things—the real stuff.

Sabino Alley was a long and narrow street and very winding. Only one car could be driven there at a time. The houses along that street were all made of adobe, but they were tall, like they made them in the olden days. They were beautifully constructed—they had beautiful woodwork with gables and massive doors. They had *portones* or passageways where the carriages used to go through, And behind the houses there were courtyards. The houses were very beautiful— they were strong houses—and well built. That would have been a beautiful shopping area. There is so much fuss made over the Cushing Street Bar, but is nothing compared to what they knocked down. They knocked down the best on Meyer Street, on Convent Street and on Sabino Alley. Sabino Alley doesn't even exist anymore. I guess they destroyed about 50 percent of those old neighborhoods, and they destroyed the best houses.

The Otero House, for example, was a jewel and beautifully taken care of because it had remained in the family. Don Teófilo took very good care of it and so did his descendants. It had a porch all the way around it; it had a lot of beautiful furniture also. The house was never allowed to deteriorate and yet it was torn down. They tore it down because it didn't fit in with their plans. They saved the Córdova House because it just happened not to be in the way of their plans.

I remember also the beautiful houses that were on Jackson Street. The only house that was saved was the Samaniego House. It is now a restaurant. But Jackson Street does not exist anymore. I remember the Carrillo-Sosa house very well. It was right next to our store on Meyer—right across the arroyo. It was rented out for some time by the descendants of Leopoldo Carrillo. They had inherited the house. I remember that it had some very antique doors, from the style of the olden days. It had a fig tree in the back—it was a beautiful fig tree. I believe that it is still there. It is the only house in that particular area that was saved—they didn't knock it down because it just happened not to be in their way.

They had this idea that they would make the Community Center and that they would revitalize the downtown, but it didn't happen. They spent millions and millions of dollars, and look at it now. The businesses can't make it. First of all, they ran out all of the people—no one lives there anymore. No one goes to buy anything there anymore. All the shops fail. It's all fake. They would have had more success if they had left things as they were.

MARINA OLIVAS
Los Reales

My name is Marina Ruíz Olivas. I was born on March 11, 1917, in Empalme, Sonora, but I came to Tucson as a very young girl. I lived downtown on Convent Street behind the Cathedral. When I married my husband, we went to live on a little ranch by La Canoa, between here and Nogales. It was a hard life for me —I was a city girl—but I learned the life of a ranch wife. I remember that I used to have to haul all our water from Demetrio Amado's water tank. We used to work very hard.

Anyway, we chose this style of life. When we decided to buy this land, Mr. John DeLeon helped us—he was a lawyer and a judge at that time, and he is still living although he is a very old man now. He told us he would help us in whatever way he could, and so when we decided to buy this property, he helped us obtain title. He helped us with the papers and we bought this land from the county for taxes. No one else was interested in buying this property, but God helped us, and we bought it.

This area is called Los Reales, and it is part of an old Mexican settlement from the time that Arizona was a part of Mexico. I know that there is an old cemetery over there where there are headstones that date in the 1800s. Only one or two headstones are from the 1900s. That old cemetery doesn't exist anymore. When the developers bought the land they didn't let people know what their plans were. People didn't have time to protest or to even remove the remains of their ancestors. The cemetery was bulldozed and they built the houses right over it. It should have been saved, because it was a very historical place.

When we first bought this property, we could still see the ruins of the old Mexican settlement. There were ruins very close to where we built our house, and there were ruins farther down where there was a store and where the main runway for the horses was. There were old wells and ruins of humble adobe houses. The adobes were by that time just mounds of dirt, but you could see that they had been buildings at one time. We have never dug to look for things, but when it rains and some of the topsoil washes away, we have found small things, like a pin or a brooch or a spoon. When we moved here we had to fill up the old wells with dirt because we worried that our children might fall into them. Actually, the wells were not terribly deep, because in the old days the water was very close to the surface and they did not have to dig too deep.

Did you know that right over there, where the bridge is on the highway—on the south side of the highway, by that little hill—there used to be a beautiful spring there, an artesian well. All the Papago and Mexican families used to picnic there. It was so beautiful. There were beautiful cottonwood trees. It was an exquisite place. Our children used to play and bathe there. I don't know why there isn't any water there anymore—some people say it is because so many wells have been dug and all the water has been used up. The trees have disappeared also—you know that cottonwood trees need a lot of water. But on the old Los Reales Road you can still see the huge old stumps of the old cottonwood trees that have died for lack of water. They were immense and beautiful things.

I remember we used to come on foot all the way from town to make a *manda* (petition) at the Mission. The manda tradition comes from the other side— Mexico—but a lot of people from this area make devotions to San Francisco. The manda continues from generation to generation. You can still see people here along the freeway in the early morning—sometimes at three in the morning—on their way to making a manda to San Xavier Mission. It is easier for them to go now on the freeway frontage road than along the old way, Indian Valley Road. That's where the huge old cottonwoods used to be, and we used to stop and rest under those trees on the way from doing errands or on the way to the Mission.

We used to own all that area that is now frontage road for the freeway. We used to farm all the way up to the river. But the freeway divided what we had. We sold our land to the state—all that frontage—we sold to the state for $1,000 for the right of way. And you see those big power lines going through our property by our fields? We fought against that. But you know, you think that something belongs to you, but when the government wants to do something, they do it no matter what you say. When you're poor, you have no power against the government.

We have a few cattle and hogs still. We used to have dairy cattle too—we milked them and I made cheese. I would make *quesadillas* (tortillas with melted cheese) and sell them. But it's not worth it anymore because no one wants to buy our cheese. People don't seem to appreciate that kind of quality any longer. They have become used to other things and they say that supermarket cheese is better than homemade cheese.

We have about seven hogs right now. We slaughter them at Christmas for tamales. People come to buy the pork when we have it. The inspector says there is no better meat than what we raise. We don't feed our animals any chemicals. My husband still slaughters the cattle and I dress all the meat. They slaughter over there in the corral and then skin it and wash it and hang it. It takes me about a day and a half to dress the meat—I cut it up and make steaks or hamburgers or *carne seca* (beef jerky) or whatever. I cook beans with beef bones—they are really delicious that way. You know, an onion and a beef bone or two—there's nothing better than beans cooked that way. And a little piece of our meat cooked over the coals is better than any fancy steak you can buy at the supermarket.

My husband built this house. We have never had any heating or cooling system—just the heat from the wood stove in the winter and the breezes in the summer. Up until last year, that is. We put in that fireplace. I have a gas stove now, but I prefer using my wood stove to make tortillas. They just seem to come out better that way.

So this is how we have lived. We have always been fortunate. We have been poor, but God has always been good to us.

FELIX OLIVAS
Los Reales

My name is Felix Olivas. I was born in 1900 in Tubac, Arizona. That's where I was raised. My parents had a little ranch in the area called Rancho Chavez. They owned their own land and for all I know there might be some ruins left of the house where we used to live. My father's name was José Olivas, and my mother's name was Josefa Salcido Olivas. They were born in Sonora, but they were pioneer Arizonans. After a time they moved from Rancho Chavez to an area across from La Canoa Ranch where they homesteaded. They homesteaded about a section and a half. The name of the ranch was Rancho Amargosa. We had a few cattle at the ranch—about a hundred head—and we also farmed. Mr. Manning, who was the owner of La Canoa Ranch, used to let us use his bulls for stud. He was a very rich man and owned thousands of acres and thousands of cattle. I lived at the Rancho Amargosa from about 1915 to 1932. In 1932, the year I was married, my wife and I settled in the same area where we had our own little ranch. I understand that that land is worth a great deal of money now, but I sold it for almost nothing.

In 1937 my wife and I moved to the Tucson area and bought land from Luís Bustamante who was the executor of the estate of Antonio Bustamante. We bought nineteen acres and later sold it to an American woman who later sold it to San Xavier Rock and Sand. After we sold our nineteen acres, we bought this land where we are now. We bought about thirty acres. We have some of the land— giving about ten acres to our sons. One of our sons, Pete, is building that house that you see over there. We have given some of the land to our grandchildren, and I believe we have about fifteen acres left.

There aren't many people here now in the Los Reales area, but I understand that in the old days—in the 1800s that is—there were a lot of Mexican families

"So this is how we have lived... We have been poor, but God has always been good to us."

living here. This used to be quite a farming and ranching area—I understand that the farmers planted a lot of wheat. But then, in the old days, there was a lot more water. The Santa Cruz River had a lot of water and it used to run all year round. Anyway, it was a very ancient settlement, but by the time we bought this land, Los Reales was all abandoned. When we bought this property, we were the only ones here, and we have been the only ones here who have been ranching.

We have lived here for forty-four years, and I have been a farmer and a rancher all of my life. I am eighty years old, and I am still farming. Today, just before you came, I was planting corn. It won't be ready until late summer, but then, when the people going by on the freeway see that the corn is ready, they stop to buy.

I also plant watermelon, chiles, tomatoes and Mexican squash in the summer and people stop to buy them too.

I have a few cattle and a bull and a few little calves. My brand is O Bar F. I also raise a few hogs. I grew everything for my family and my farm used to be bigger while I was raising my family. We had ten children. Now, of course, it isn't necessary to raise so much, but I guess I'll just keep going. Up until five years ago I still plowed with mules and a horse, but now I am too old. My boys think that it is too difficult for me the old-fashioned way and they come and help me plow with a tractor. But I never cared much for tractors—you know how they are always breaking down. I still like to use my hoe and I still do some of the work by hand.

I built this house we live in. It is adobe. I made the adobes myself the old-fashioned way with mud and straw. And I dug my own well here. I dug it with a pick and shovel. It was forty-five feet deep. But the deepest well I ever dug was on the Rancho Amargosa—it was eighty-five to one hundred feet deep, and my brother and I dug it all by hand. Now I am pumping water with an electric pump and that's how I get the water for my farming.

Anyway, my children aren't interested in this kind of life. They don't care much for the life of a ranchero—they have other jobs. It's so different now—my children earn so much! A thousand dollars a month! I remember I used to bale hay for $1.50 a day, working from sunup to sunset. Now it takes so much more to live.

FRANK ESCALANTE

& The Far East Side & The Rincons

My name is Frank Escalante. I was born right here on this ranch fifty-eight years ago. But our history goes back much farther than that. My grandparents on both sides came from Ures, Sonora, Mexico. I am not sure exactly when, but I know that it was over 100 years ago. My grandmother used to tell stories of the Gold Rush of 1849, so that's how I know. My dad's grandfather is buried in Ures. He was a general in the Spanish army. His wife and children came here to keep from being executed during the war against Spain.

Anyway, my grandfather's name was Manuel Escalante. He married Dolores Lauterio. They had twenty-five children. He had a brother named Miguel—he was one of the more prosperous Escalantes. He owned a ranch near Gates Pass. Eventually he went into business with Steinfeld and became a big landowner.

At one time there were Escalantes all over the Rincon Mountains. My grandfather was an all-around man—a jack-of-all-trades, you might say. He worked wherever work came up. You know where El Rancho del Lago is? He used to farm in that area with my Dad—over here by Vail. But don't go there. They have cut down all the cottonwoods. They have bulldozed everything.

He worked for the forest service when they started the monument.* In 1904, I think it was, the surveyors sent my granddad up to Mica Mountain. He took cement and made a marker up there. He also took the first wagon up on Rincon Peak when the National Forest Boundary line had been made. He took a stove up there to the lookout tower.

---

*Saguaro National Monument East, at the foot of the Rincon Mountains, is within the Coronado National Forest.

Bienvenidos—welcome.

My grandfather used to work on the lime kilns also. My dad used to help him when he was a boy. The lime kilns are made of mud and rock. You can find them all over these mountains. Someday I'll show you one. They used to get a certain kind of rock, see. They would fill the kiln with rocks and wood. The wood would burn for a day or two and separate the lime from the rock. Then they would bring the lime into town to sell to the builders. In fact, that's how my grandfather died. He was bringing in bags of lime in a wagon. The Pantano was running and the wagon got stuck. My grandfather began to carry off the bags of lime to lighten the load. And he had a heart attack. An uncle of mine who was then a boy went for help. He came back with a cowboy and they took the body home.

My dad originally homesteaded what is now known as Loma Alta Road. But when he got married he sold that place out there because he wanted to move closer to my mom's folks. He sold his land on Loma Alta for $600. He only collected $400. Do you know what that land is selling for now? $14,000 an acre. Anyway, my mom's name was Florentina Moreno. Her folks had a ranch right next to this place. They had 140 acres right off of Harrison Road. They grazed stock all over what is now Davis-Monthan Air Force Base.

As I said, I was born here on this very ranch. My dad homesteaded 160 acres here in 1919. I was born right over there. My mom used to tell this story. She was working in the fields when it was time for me to be born. She felt the pains. She took the team and tied it to a paloverde tree. Then she walked to the house where she said I just dropped. She cut the cord and tied it and then she set me on a blanket. Then she thought of the horses tied up out there in the heat. She went out to the field and brought them in and then she came in to clean me up. That's the way my mother was. She could work like a man and nothing fazed her. She did all the plowing and the breaking of the horses.

The house that I was born in was not like houses now. What people did was this. They would find a big mesquite. They would use cardboard and tin and make the walls and cover them with mud. And they would use saguaro ribs or ocotillo for the roof. That's the kind of home I was born in. I have a picture of it. They used to hang my cradle from a chain between the mesquite posts. I still have the chain that they used to hang my cradle. I still have the post.

The ranch life was all I knew as a child. We had cattle and we used to grow everything—wheat, barley, milo, oats. We raised our own food—corn, beans, chiles, lentils, watermelons, different kinds of vegetables. We even grew tobacco. My dad used to make his own cigars. We were self-sufficient. My mother made

Heirlooms.

cheese from the milk. She used to dry food, too. She made beef jerky. The real kind—not the kind you find now that is dried in the oven. When we were children we used to help her collect the fruit from saguaros and she would make jams and jellies. We had our own beehives and had honey. When the Depression came, we didn't even know it.

We used to irrigate from the Pantano. When it rained we used to take the teams down there and load barrels of water. We would haul our drinking water from a well four miles away. When it rained we filled everything we could with the runoff. We would filter the tadpoles out with a cloth. Then we would have good drinking water. For a refrigerator, we would stand up four poles and make shelves. My mom would hang gunnysacks on them. There was always a barrel of water there and everytime we'd pass we'd sprinkle the gunnysacks. It was just a habit.

Whatever crops we didn't use ourselves from the farm, we would take into town and sell. We used to take a load of wood also. We just loved to see the Pantano flood, because there was a lot of driftwood that would come down. We would pick it up out of the wash and load it in a wagon and sell it in town. I would leave here at four o'clock in the morning with a load of wood. I'd go to Convent and Main. That's where the Community Center is now. I'd sell a load of wood for $1.50. The most we could get was $1.75, but that was darn good money. We used to be in competition with the Papago Indians because they would bring wood into town to sell also.

I used to leave the horses at a stable that belonged to Manuel Elías on Main Street. Chinatown used to be right opposite the stables. They would water and feed the horses for the day for twenty-five cents. I would get back from town about eight o'clock at night. By the time I got back my dad had another load. And then I'd take another load in the morning. I was hauling wood to town from here when I was about ten years old. That would have been around 1933.

I still have a lot of the old equipment that we used to use on the ranch. I still have parts of that old wagon. I guess you could say that I am sentimental. For example, the *fresno*—the buck rake. My Dad bought it from Ronstadt's in 1925 and I still have it here out by my front fence. In fact, some students came over from the university about ten years ago. I don't know how they found out about it. Anyway, you can't find that old-time stuff anymore. They wanted to take it. I told them they could take all the pictures they wanted. So they did. "Would you sell it to us?" one of them asked me. "No, Ma'am," I said. "I can't sell it." She asked me why. "Because it has a lot of sentimental value," I told her. "You mean to tell me," she says, "that if I offered you $5,000 for that piece of junk that you wouldn't sell it to me?" "Ma'am," I says, "you can offer me $50,000 and I wouldn't sell it to you. It's just the idea that it belonged to my dad."

I've saved a lot of other things too. There by the door is my mother's old *mano** that she used for grinding corn. Out on the porch of my son's house I've nailed up a lot of things. I've got the old stuff—coyote and fox traps, bridles, rifles, branding irons, an old wooden pack saddle. Even one of my mom's old cooking pans. I've got some old cavalry stirrups that used to belong to my uncle. He used to haul grain from Huachuca to Fort Lowell. I don't know how some of that stuff hasn't fallen down by now. It's been nailed up there so long. I've got more old tools welded out there onto a fence. I've even got my mom's old iron bed. My son is going to fix it up someday.

Anyway, as I have told you, the ranch life was all I knew as a kid. I went to school, of course. I went to the school on Wrightstown Road. At that time it was just one room about the size of this living room. It went up to the sixth grade. I used to have to walk from here to Golf Links and Pantano to catch the bus because that's as far as the bus would come. Sometimes I would miss the bus and then I'd have to walk all the way to school. I wouldn't get to school until 9:30. I used to run through the desert—there wasn't anyone living there at that time except the Garrigans. When I started school I spoke only Spanish. I didn't even know how to ask to go to the restroom in English. It was rough.

You know, in my day, we didn't have any affirmative action or minority rights or whatever you call it. I went through hell and high water to make something of myself on my own. But I have no regrets. The service did a lot for me. During the Second World War, I was an artillery spotter. I walked across France to Germany. I trained with an outfit of 150 men. When the war ended there were only nine of us alive. When they were going to invade Japan, I was part of a combat unit. We were getting ready to embark at Antwerp when the war was over.

So then I decided to stay with the Army of Occupation. I started working with the railroad and from there as an interpreter for the military government. That's when I met my wife, in Austria. Then I started school. I was going to school from six to eleven o'clock at night. I was taking welding, automotive mechanics and painting. It was another world for me. When I left for the service I hardly knew

---

*A *mano* is a hand held stone used for grinding corn for making tortillas. It is used with a mortar, or *metate*.

what a car was. All I had ever done was ride horseback. That's what I mean, you see. A man can make something of himself if he wants to. Before I went, all I knew was farming, selling wood, waiting for roundup, going out to some ranch that had some fencebuilding to do. But you can't survive like that anymore. You can't make it.

I could have stayed in Austria, but I decided to come home because of the old folks. So when I came back I went to the Arizona School of Aeronautics. Then I got a job at Davis-Monthan where I worked for fourteen and a half years. In 1953 I was working on a plane. I jumped down on the wing and landed with my knee out of alignment. I had to have the knee operated on and finally I had to retire on disability. Then I got a job working on county roads. The job lasted for fourteen years. But my knee got worse and worse. I just got out of the hospital from another knee operation. And no one wants to hire someone with a bum knee because they're afraid he'll have an accident.

And I can't make it ranching. My dad, though, had this life until he died. He had cattle until the day he died. In fact, he was feeding them when he died. He died in 1967. He lived to be eighty-four years old. When he died he left me and my sisters twenty acres each. Two of my sisters, Consuelo Sánchez and Petra Laras, lived just east of me. Another one of my sisters, Manuela Krampel, lives just to the southeast, behind that ocotillo fence on Irvington. My dad helped build those houses. And I have three sons living here on what's left of the old homestead. One lives over there in our old house. Another lives in that doublewide trailer beside the house. Another lives down the dirt road a piece. Of all my sons, though, only one has followed the ranch life. His name is Richard. He was state bull riding champ in 1976.

The boys and I built this house with stuff from the dump. We used to go to the dump and pick up block. And the adobe—I bought it from a fellow who had it stacked near his house for I don't know how many years. I think I gave him twenty-five dollars for the whole shebang. I made the porch roof from some lumber from an old bridge. I found that weeping mulberry at the dump. I've never seen another one like it. All that grass you see out there is from a small clump I picked up at a shopping center.

But I don't know. As I told you I stay here on the old place just because I'm sentimental. It's in my blood, I guess. I can't get used to city life. I've had to sell some of my land to pay for hospital expenses. I've only got five acres left. And I've only got 104 acres left of the land I leased from the state. The government took

This land is ours.

forty acres of my leased land for a dump. And now they've raised their fees on me. I built those stables out there so I could board horses. I invested $12,000 in those stables. And now I can't afford the leased land. They changed the leased land from grazing to commercial. My rates went from $600 a year to $1700 a year. Now the stables are so much junk. I can't even graze the few cattle I have anymore.

I went up to Phoenix to the land department and I told them, "Look, I'm not a revolutionary or a communist or anything. I'm just a man who is looking for a little respect for his efforts." But they keep giving me the runaround. I don't know what I'm going to do. I know they just want me out of here—they are trying to force me off. Look at all those houses out there. The developers want me out so they can have my land. The guy at the land department told me, "If you don't like it, why don't you just drop your leases." "Because I'm not going to give you the satisfaction," I told him. They told me that the reason they raised my fees is because I'm close to IBM. "Oh, cut it out," I said. "There's 100,000 acres between me and IBM." I'll tell you what it is. All that land east of Kolb Road and south of Stella used to belong to the state. Look who's got it now. Developers. Look at that mess—all those houses across the wash. I'm surrounded now. And here I am. What's the population of Tucson now? 500,000. And who is going to pay attention to me? The United States is supposed to be helping human rights all over the world and yet right here in your own backyard they stomp on you.

And that's why sometimes I say I feel like selling. Because I can't hack it. I'll never be a city slicker. Maybe I'll move out to Cochise County. Get me another little ranch. Some people can change and some people can't. Sentimentality doesn't seem to exist anymore. It's the dollar that counts.

It's happened before. You know out here from this mountain to that mountain, from the Rincons to the Catalinas used to be owned by Mexicans and what happened to all of them. I can name you names—the Estradas, the Andrades, the Vindiolas, the Lopez. I have a book that I can show you. It has the names of the old Mexican ranchers in this area and their brands. The Riesgos, the Benitez, the Telles, the Martinez, the Gallegos. The list goes on and on.

And I can tell you what happened. I don't want you to think that I am prejudiced, but the facts are the facts. The rich have always stomped on the poor. I know some people who had more than 300 acres of land this side of the mountain. They worked for a rancher who told them that because they worked for him, he would pay the taxes on their land. And when he paid their taxes, he told them to get off the land. Just like that.

The adobe of the Vindiola homestead melts back into the desert floor.

The same thing happened to the Vindiolas and other people. Do you know the Vindiolas' little adobe down in the valley? My sister was born there in 1918. That little house is still standing. The well they built is still there and also an old lime kiln. It must be almost a hundred years old. Someday I can show you. My grand-dad and my dad used to work on that old lime kiln together. They used to help each other out. Some men would bring the rocks and some of the wood. And some would take a load into town.

My dad used to tell me some stories about how some of the people were said to have lost their land. For instance, the Arizona Rangers.* You remember how famous they used to be? Well, it's said they had a little trick. Say first someone wanted a little ranch. He'd go up to the ranch and put hides in the corral and then accuse the man of rustling. My mom's dad used to live on the León's Ranch above Loma Alta where it happened. He knew a man it happened to. But the man was wise to what the Rangers were up to, and when he found he was surrounded he crawled away from the ranch. He went to my grandfather's to borrow a horse. They shod the horse by lantern light. He wrote to my grandfather later that by sunrise he was in Santa Cruz, Mexico. He had to forfeit his land, but if he had stayed he would have been hanged.

The Arizona Rangers did the same thing to my dad's dad. They put hides in his corral and accused him of rustling. But Tom Richey the attorney was the one who saved my grandfather. He was Miguel Escalante's attorney and he helped my grandfather out.

My dad and other ranchers used to tell another story. There were a couple of brothers who were ranching in Rosemont over there by Sonoita. And for some reason someone wanted their land. Probably the mining. There was a lot of mining in that area. Someone must have wanted those claims. So they went and put a couple of horses in their pasture. And you know, in those days they could hang you for stealing horses. So the two brothers were coming back from Vail. One of them had just gotten married to one of the León girls. The wedding fiesta had lasted three days. And the Rangers caught them right there as they were coming out of the canyon and they hanged both of them.

I don't go for discrimination. I am just trying to tell you what I know and what my dad told me. I have lots of Anglo friends that I can really depend on. I can say to

---

*The Arizona Rangers were created as a vigilante force by the Territorial Legislature in 1901. The frontier sense of justice that prevailed undoubtedly produced abuses of power.

La Reina de las Américas—the Queen of the Americas

them, "Hey, I need $1,000" or "I need your help" and they would be out here right now. But I learned the hard way. I went through hell in the service. In Texas I couldn't even buy a cup of coffee. The facts are facts.

You know the old Rincon Cemetery out there on Old Spanish Trail? I go up there everytime I get a chance. The cemetery is before my time. Some of the graves are new but a lot of them are oldtimers. My grandfather, Manuel Escalante, is buried there. He was forty-seven when he died and he died in 1910 so that means he was born in 1863. My great uncle Miguel Escalante is buried there also and my grandmother, Dolores Lauterio Escalante. My dad and mom are buried there and a brother and a little sister. Those of us who are from around here and have folks buried there go out on All Souls Day. We light candles and have a Mass and fix up the graves.

We have a Cemetery Association to help keep up the cemetery. We used to raise money by having barbecues and rodeos. Last time we raised $4300. Sometimes we would get as many as a thousand people for one of those barbecues. But I don't have them anymore because there was too much going on and I was afraid of a lawsuit. Anyway, with the money we raised we put in a concrete slab and benches and a ramada at the cemetery. We painted the wall around the cemetery and put in a driveway. I made a luminous cross for the cemetery gate out of nuts and bolts. It lights your way in the dark.

My mom used to tell this story. She was plowing the field. She had a horse and a mule hitched together. She was breaking the horse to the plow. Then the pains came. No one was home. We were all at school and my dad was off hauling sand and gravel. She left the field and delivered the child herself. It was a boy and it was born dead. She got a flour sack and put the baby's body in it. Then she dug the grave herself and buried him. She told me where she buried him. The grave is over there across the wash where the red brick house is with the tile roof. I have been trying to find my brother's grave. I have looked for it myself and I have hired men to dig for it. I want to find it before I leave. I want to find my baby brother's grave and move it to the family burial place in the Rincon Cemetery with the rest of the Escalantes.

MARGARITA MARTINEZ
Along the Río Santa Cruz

My name is Margarita Martínez. My father's name was Manuel Valdez. He was born in Hermosillo, but his mother brought him here a very young child. That would be in the mid-1800s. Arizona was still part of Mexico in those days. As a young man, my father worked in the mines in the Santa Rita Mountains—they used to have gold mines up there, and there were a lot of Mexican families living in that area. But after he was married and the first child was born, he moved down from the mines and came to settle in Los Reales.

Los Reales was a little *ranchito* that was located at the foot of the little mountain near San Xavier Mission. It is still called Los Reales, but it is full of houses now—the city has spread all the way out there. It's not a ranch anymore.

We went to school at San Xavier. The school was near the *barranco* (riverbank). I remember the name of the teacher. Her name was Miss Martin. She used to come to town in her horse and buggy to give lessons. We were taught to read. She used to get mad when we spoke Spanish.

I remember my friend, Concepción Burruel, was being courted by Jesus María Quiroz. I used to pass notes between them by hiding them in my hat. My mother would tell me not to get involved. And I would say, "I am not carrying the notes. The hat is carrying them." It wasn't proper, you know, in those days, to speak to your beau directly.

I was born on the ranchito at Los Reales on June 11, 1890. My brother and sister were born there also, and that's where we were raised. My father was a *sembrador*—a planter or sower. There were *milpas* all along the river between San Xavier and the town, and that's where he used to work. I used to help him when I was a child. I used to help mark the holes where the rows of corn would be planted. So many feet—one plant; so many feet—another plant; and so on. And at the end of the season, when harvest time came, the man who owned the land would pay me by giving me a sack of corn.

When I was a very small child my grandmother used to live in town on 11th Street. It was just a *mesquital* in those days—a grove of mesquite trees. My grandmother earned her living by washing clothes for other people. That's how she maintained herself so that her children could go to school. I used to help her also. My mother would tell me, "Go with your grandmother so she won't be all alone because she is getting on in years." She used to wash in the river. Many, many women would gather there—they would wash clothes on the rocks. There were lots of dried branches along the river and with those dried branches they would make little fires and boil the clothes. They would make a little bag and put in the leaves of the *batamote* (seep willow). And the clothes would come out white, white. Then they would hang the clothes in the branches of the mesquite and the other bushes that grew along the river.

My grandmother was here when the first train arrived. She used to wash for the families of the men who worked for the railroad—laying the track. Those families were poor, but not as poor as the rest of us, because they had regular paying jobs. After the day's work was done, my grandmother would say to me, "*Vámonos, mijita. Vamos a llevar la ropa.*" "Come on, my little daughter. We shall go and deliver the clothes." And she would tie up the day's wash in a bundle and we would take the bundle with the clean clothing and deliver it to the families. On the way, we would pass the flour mill. The flour mill had doors above and a scale below. That's where they would put the sacks of wheat to weigh them. They grew wheat along the river in those days. Some people would buy large amounts, and some people would buy small amounts. We would always buy a little sack of wheat for the hens and the little chicks. We always had fresh eggs, and I was used to that. But then the Americans came, and I guess they don't like chickens because they always buy their eggs in a box.

There was in the old days a little house along the river. It was before you get to Callejón Carrillo. They used to say that the man and woman and their children who used to live there used to make adobes to sell. They had a little well and they used to haul their water out with a wheel and pulley and rope. Of course, when I was little, the house was no longer there—there was nothing left of the well or the pulley. And the ladies who used to wash at the river used to say, "*Vámonos temprano, antes de que se aparezca el espanto.*" ("Let's go home early, before the ghost appears.") As soon as it gets dark, you will be able to see a woman's ghost. She is taking water out of the well and then you can hear pulleys squeak and make noise." And they could hear the water sloshing around in the bucket. And everyone was very much afraid.

I remember the old Mission Church of San Cosme. There were a few ruins left—huge stones and adobes. There was a small room that was still standing. I remember how it looked—it had only one entrance. People used to say that there was buried treasure there. There was a woman who had divining rods which she used to look for the gold. She would hire out men so that they could dig for the treasure in those rooms. My husband didn't care to join in the search. He used to say, "When you're poor, you're poor, and when you're rich, you're rich. Don't look for that which you have not lost."

The little house that my husband and I built still stands. It is on Melwood Street. My son still lives there. We had a little milpa there—not far from the river, and we used to plant with the will of God. When the season for planting was over, my husband would go and work in the dairy. That way we would have money for food and other necessities until the harvest. We would plant beans and corn and squash and watermelon. We have a picture of one of the pumpkins that we grew on our little milpa—it was huge. Later, when the railroad came through, they bought that little piece of land that we had.

You know, when I was young, we were very innocent and simple—not like the young people of today. We used to believe everything. An old man, the brother of my father-in-law, told us that story of La Llorona.* I never heard her or saw her, but I used to use the story to make my children behave when they wouldn't go to sleep at night. I used to tell them, "Quiet down, or La Llorona will come and get you." Anyway, the old man said that La Llorona had been a wicked girl. She would have "babitos" (little babies) and she didn't know what to do with them. And so she would throw them in the river and drown them. She had already had seven children when she died. And "Tatadios"** would not let her into heaven. He made her return to earth and gather her children out of the river,

*The story of La Llorona, or the Wailing Woman, is a classic Mexican legend dating to the time of the Conquest. Some scholars maintain that it is based on La Malinche, the Indian mistress of Cortez. Hundreds of local variations on the tale occur, and the story is often used to frighten recalcitrant children into behaving. In the Tucson area the story has a particularly interesting variant: it is believed that La Llorona is heard when the Santa Cruz River is flowing.

**"Tatadios" is a term of respect referring to God as a grandfatherly figure.

"We used to plant with the will of God."

because that's where she had drowned them. And she cannot go to heaven until she finds all her children. And that is why she cries and wails—because she is looking for her children, and she cannot go to heaven until she finds all her children. I don't believe that it is her real body that is wandering; I believe it must be her soul—her spirit. And when the Santa Cruz River floods, that's when she is supposed to cry.

On this side of the Carrillo Gardens—on the corner of Main—they made a salon for dancing and skating. I didn't like for my children to go and skate because they were always falling down and hurting themselves. The mayor of the town—I can't remember his name—didn't like the salon because he didn't like the fact that so many were gathered together in one place. He told the Mexican people that something bad was going to happen there. Well, one night the young people began to say that they didn't want to go to the salon anymore because they had heard that the devil had appeared there. I said, "Good! Now you won't want to go to the dances or skating anymore!" Sometimes the devil can be a help to us mothers! Anyway, the story goes that one night everyone was dancing when a ballerina came in through the window of the salon. She was dressed in a very strange manner—in a short dancing dress. Everyone was very surprised. An object like a ball of sulfur followed her through the window—it had no features—no face or eyes. And the dance hall was filled with the smell of sulfur and everyone had to leave. The girl disappeared, but after that the skating and dancing were finished. Everyone was afraid to go there.

Anyway, there were always a lot of stories like that. Some you believe and others you don't. But you never really know for sure.

MIGUEL AMADO
Amado, Arizona

My name is Miguel Amado. I was born in 1905 in Amado, Arizona. My father's name was Demetrio Amado and my mother's name was Carmen Celaya de Amado. My father was born in Tucson and my mother was born in Atil, Sonora. Atil is in the district of Altar. My grandparents' names were Manuel Amado and Ismaela Amado. My grandfather came to Tucson from Hermosillo in 1850. So you see, my family has been in this area for a long time—for over a hundred years. My grandchildren are now the fifth generation.

In the era of my grandparents, farming and ranching were the most common thing that people did for a living. My grandfather, Manuel, had a contract with the government of the United States to bring grain from Sáric, Sonora, to Fort Lowell. He has a ranch near Tubac* in what is now Santa Cruz County. The ranch was called *El Alamo Bonito* (The Beautiful Cottonwood).

Before that they were ranching near San Xavier.** It was an area called Los Reales and many of the old-time Mexican families ranched in that place. My grandparents had a dairy there and they also made cheese. When the San Xavier Reservation was made, the people were run off the land. Their corrals and their little houses were burned. I guess it must have been the government agents who did it.

---

*Tubac, located approximately 40 miles south of Tucson, was established as an army presidio by Spain in 1752. Later a pueblo and mission settlement grew up around the fort. Tubac is now an Arizona State Park.

**San Xavier Mission was founded by Father Kino in the early 18th century for the Papago Indians. Located nine miles south of Tucson in the Santa Cruz River Valley, it is a famous Tucson landmark and is known as La Paloma del Desierto, The Dove of the Desert. It is thought to be the oldest mission in Arizona and California.

And that is when they moved to Amado. They went there and claimed their land. There were not many families in that valley at that time and when someone claimed a portion of land the claim was respected. There were no fences in those days. Our cattle ran all the way from Amado to Tucson, from Nogales to Cortaro. So we are talking about a lot of territory.

My grandparents had a big family—there were ten or eleven children. When they were grown all the children staked a claim in that area and so the family holdings grew. The town was eventually named for the family. In the old days it was known as Amadoville. I remember that all the children—my father and my aunts and uncles all built houses close to the old man's place, El Alamo Bonito.

When the old people died, the children divided the property and the cattle. They all got their share—the girls as well. Each of them ended up with a ranch; they each got nine sections. So you see, we are talking about a lot of land. When they divided the cattle and the horses they had a raffle. That is, they drew lots so that the livestock would be divided fairly. Some of the horses were very fine horses; they were very valuable. And so that was the fair way to do it. By luck of the draw.

The oldest son, my Tío Manuel, inherited the original ranch, El Alamo Bonito. It is about a mile north of the town of Amado. But El Alamo Bonito no longer belongs to the family. It has been sold many times and now belongs to a family by the name of Middleton.

There was a church on the Alamo Bonito Ranch. My Tío Manuel and My Tía Armida built that church. We all helped raise funds to build it and we also helped with certain phases of the construction. It had thick adobe walls. The family attended church there for many years. Even my children used to go to church there. And all the ranching people from that area came to mass there. The priest used to come from Nogales to say mass. He would go to Tubac and say mass and then he would come to our church in Amado. The church is the only part of the original ranch buildings that still exists. But it is no longer used as a church. It is now the residence of the Middletons.

My father farmed and ranched in what is now known as Amado. The ranch was very large. You know where Green Valley Desert Hills Golf Course is? Well, that used to be part of my father's land. We used to run 3,000 head of cattle up there. In 1918—I was only about thirteen or fourteen—I put in the fence up there. I used to go up there every day to tend the cattle. And if you look on an old map of that area, you will see something called Demetrio's Well and Demetrio's Wash. That was named after my father because he used to own that land.

My father built the house on the ranch where I was raised. The house was built in 1898 and my father was still living there when he died in 1956. He and a neighbor, Martín Romero, did most of the work on the house. I guess you could say that Martín Romero was the "architect." The house was made of adobe and it had an ocotillo ceiling. The kitchen and the bedrooms were on one side and the living room was on another. The living room was where the finer furniture was kept. There was a piano. The living room was locked because that was my mother's room. I remember that my father's desk was in there also. That's where he did his work. You see, my father was a college graduate. He went to Santa Clara College, a Jesuit school in California. He was a very well read and educated man.

We had a fairly large vegetable garden at the ranch and also an orchard. There was a windmill for pumping the water for irrigating. The vegetable garden was about two or three acres. My mother used to be in charge of the vegetable garden. It was very beautiful—there were many kinds of vegetables and also many beautiful flowers. I remember especially the flowers in that garden. There were so many flowers that there were paths between them. I remember especially a green flower—it was dark green with bright green branches and leaves. They used to say that my father had sent to France for it. I don't know what the name of that flower was, but I have never seen another like it. My mother used to can the fruits and vegetables. She had an *almacén,* a storeroom, to store the provisions that she had put up. It really wasn't too long ago that I saw some of the old jars with the fruit still in them. Of course everything was rotten. After my mother died it all stayed in the storeroom and was neglected.

And that area where I was raised, the property and the house that belonged to my parents, was sold not too long ago. The house was in bad condition; it was abandoned and neglected so it was torn down. The mines bought the land for water rights, so there is no one farming or ranching there anymore.

As for myself, I was born in Amado, I was raised there and I went to school there. My father was a trustee of the school and he would send away for teachers from the East. We were taught in English because the teachers were all Americans. Of course all the children spoke Spanish in those days, but we were punished for speaking it. As a matter of fact, the teachers used to live with us. They had a room in our home. They would eat breakfast with us and then we would take them to school in a horse and buggy. And then we would bring them back in the evening.

As a matter of fact, my father was the sheriff of that area. Manuel Arvizu was the judge. I guess you could say they ran the village.

"If I don't take care of the land, then who will?"

You know, I have been working ever since I can remember. When I was only about three they used to send me to sell eggs from the ranch at the first store in Amado. It was owned by Mr. Exendine, who was an American Indian. He had bought the land from my father. And when we had more vegetables than we could use from the garden, my mother would send me with a little basket to sell the vegetables to the Chinamen who had the little stores. The reason I am mentioning this is so that you can realize how small I was when I began working.

I remember when I was about five years old, an uncle of mine came from Altar to ship the cattle from Amado. That's where the stockyards were. There was no other loading place in those days, except Amado. The cattle would be shipped from there to the west coast. When my uncle's cattle from Altar were loaded on the train, all the cowboys who had been on the cattle drive embarked on the train also in order to accompany the cattle on the journey. So their horses had to be taken back to Mexico. I rode back to Altar with my uncle to help take back the horses. You know, I was very small to have made such a long trip on horseback. It took us three days and two nights. I remember that after the first day, the horse was trotting so much that my stomach was aching. So my uncle bandaged me with his *bufanda* (scarf) girdle-like so that the trotting of the horse wouldn't jar my insides. And then we traded horses and continued on the trip to Atil.

I think I must have been riding since the day I was born. I was raised on a horse. That's all there was in those days. So everyone rode. If you weren't in a wagon, you were on a horse.

I remember also, that when I was a very small boy my Tío Manuel at the Alamo Bonito would pay me to mark the ears of the calves. That is a way of cutting the ear of the calf so that it can be identified. I would slice off a little tip of the ear to mark the calf and I would take the little pieces to my uncle and he would pay me for however many I had. Now I'm not talking about paper money the way it is today. I am talking about gold coins.

I guess I wanted to help my uncle because he was very busy with his other business. He had a store there at the ranch. It was the only one of its kinds in the area. People used to come from as far away as Sonora to buy supplies from him. It was quite a large business. He sold everything you could think of: saddles, harness, tack, and clothing.

I have seen a lot of changes in the area but I really don't believe things have gotten better. The freeway has cut right through there and you can't even notice Amado from the highway any more. Now in the part that they call Amado, you can pass there and not see a single person. There used to be three stores there and a train depot and a pool hall. Now not a single family lives out there any more. All the old ranching families have gone.

One of my neighbors used to be Don Gabino Grijalva. He used to have a little claim up there next to my land. But when the war [World War I] came, he didn't want his sons to go, so he went to Nogales, Sonora. The land was abandoned and so the bank took over. Also millionaires have bought the old ranch lands. You know, for an investment and for tax purposes. One of the ranches is owned by some millionaires who live in Italy. They have someone staying on their property but they never come there. But mostly it's the mines who own everything now. When the mines bought the land for the water rights, they razed everything. Wells, pumps, houses, everything. They don't want to be bothered with any of the old buildings.

I moved my family to Tucson in 1950 so that my children could get a better education. I have a house in town. But I have always stayed with the ranch. I get up at five every morning. I leave for the ranch around seven or eight and work until it is dark. I get home around nine or ten. I do this every day of the week. I work alone out at the ranch. I have cattle there and hayfields. I have to take care of my cattle. If I don't take care of them, who will? I do everything myself. I rope, I brand, I dehorn them and mark their ears. I castrate them myself. I feed them. On Fridays I bring the cattle in to the auction. The inspector comes down to look over the stock. After they are inspected I load them and truck them in myself. As for the rest of the ranch, I have to mend fences. There is always so much work to do. I have to cultivate and bale the hay and run the tractor. Sometimes I have to go to Casa Grande for parts to repair the machinery at the ranch. I usually leave Casa Grande about noon but I still go to the ranch.

I used to plant every kind of vegetable. I planted my father's land with all kinds of potatoes. I was known as the king of produce. Now I just plant a few acres for my children. I plant white corn, green chiles, and squash for them. It keeps me busy, I can tell you.

I guess I am one of the last of the oldtimers out there who still has land and works it. The ranch life is a hard life. My children have experienced that life. But now they have other opportunities. They have had a chance to educate themselves and they have worked hard and done well. But as for myself, I have to keep working on the ranch. If I don't take care of the land, then who will?